BrightRED Results

Standard Grade
ENGLISH

David Cockburn

D0177103

First published in 2008 by:
Bright Red Publishing Ltd
6 Stafford Street
Edinburgh
EH3 7AU

ISBN 978-1-906736-09-5

With thanks to:
The Partnership Publishing Solutions (layout) and Project One Publishing Solutions (copy-edit)

Author acknowledgements
I should like to thank first of all the Bright Red Publishing team, whose care and attention to detail are a delight to any author. I should also like to acknowledge my indebtedness and gratitude to Peter Doughty, Chief Examiner of English at OCR, as well as Patsy Musto, formerly Director of French Encounters, whose knowledge about grammar and language is almost limitless. And finally and most importantly, I want to thank Kevin Cockburn for all his enthusiasm, encouragement, and endless patience.

Cover design by Caleb Rutherford – e i d e t i c

Illustrations by Armadillo Jam

Every effort has been made to seek all copyright holders. If any have been overlooked then Bright Red Publishing will be delighted to make the necessary arrangements.

Acknowledgements
Bright Red Publishing would like to make the following acknowledgements for permission to reproduce extracts within this text.
Extract adapted from the article 'Blinded by the Stars' by John Harlow, from page 16 of The Sunday Times, August 17th 2003. Reproduced by kind permission of News International; Extracts from Watching Mrs Gordon and Other Stories (Bodley Head Ltd) © Ronald Frame 1985; Extracts from Atonement by Ian McEwan, published by Jonathan Cape. Reprinted by permission of The Random House Group Ltd; Extract from Captain Correlli's Mandolin by Louis de Bernieres, published by Secker & Warburg. Reprinted by permission of The Random House Group Ltd; Extract from The Ode Less Travelled, by Stephen Fry, published by Hutchinson. Reprinted by permission of David Higham Associates Ltd; Extracts adapted from the article 'The Fabulous Biker Boys (and Girls)' by John Dodd, taken from the Sunday Telegraph Magazine, 28 August 2005. Reproduced by permission of The Telegraph Media Group Limited; Extract from Impact - The Threat of Comets and Asteroids by Verschuur, Gerrit L. (1997). By permission of Oxford University Press, Inc; Extracts from Journeys by Morris, Jan (1985). Reproduced by permission of Oxford University Press, Inc; Extract from Asya by Michael Ignatieff, published by Chatto & Windus. Reprinted by permission of The Random House Group Ltd; Extract from an article by Melanie Reid, 'We're pedalling to a glorious new dawn Melanie Reid on Tuesday' by Melanie Reid, The Herald, 07th Nov 2006. Reproduced with permission Herald & Times Group; Extract from an article by Ruth Wishart, 'Can Britain Afford to Keep Talented Immigrants out?' The Herald, 27th June 2002. Reproduced with permission Herald & Times Group; Extract from 'Pucker Ways to Kiss a Hummingbird' by Mark Carwardine, is taken from The Mail on Sunday, 18 August 2002. Reproduced by permission of The Mail on Sunday, Solo Syndication Ltd; Extract from The Verger by W Somerset Maugham. Reproduced by permission of A P Watt Ltd on behalf of The Royal Literary Fund; Extract from Of Mice and Men by John Steinbeck, published by Penguin Classics, 2000. Reproduced by permission of The Penguin Group. 'Extracts from You Don't Know Me by David Klass. Reprinted with permission from The Aaron M. Priest Literary Agency, 2008; Extract from The Joy of Hillwalking by Ralph Storer. Reprinted with permission from Luath Press; Extract from From the Diary of a New York Lady by Dorothy Parker, from Complete Stories by Dorothy Parker, Colleen Breese, Regina Barreca. Reprinted with permission from Duckworth Publishers.

Bright Red Publishing would also like to thank the Scottish Qualifications Authority for use of Past Exam Questions. Answers do not emanate from the SQA.

Printed and bound in Scotland by Scotprint

Contents

The Standard Grade course

What does Standard Grade English involve?

Standard Grade is a two-year English course that is usually spread over third and fourth year of your Secondary schooling and results in a Credit, General, or a Foundation award. Some schools teach the course over S2 and S3, leaving more time for Higher in fifth year. If your interests lie in achieving a Credit award to see you through to your Higher course next year, then this is exactly the book for you!

The importance of literature and developing language skills

What really matters about Standard Grade is the course itself: the literature that you will study and the language skills you will practise. You will need to know:

about the three genres of English literature – **drama**, **prose** and **poetry**

how to approach the various texts that you will be presented with, and how to write a critical essay on those texts

how to compose an essay on a given subject.

You must be able to read accurately and with understanding a piece of moderately difficult prose, such as the kind you will come across in the Close Reading paper.

It is all about developing skills!

You can see right away that the course is very much skills-based: that's the nature of English. But you also need to have knowledge about the ways in which language works, and, of course, you need to have knowledge of the literature you study.

The assessment of skills

There are three aspects to the assessment of the various skills developed throughout your Standard Grade course:

1 A **Folio** of Coursework internally produced and externally assessed, submitted in the year of the examination

2 An **external examination** in Close Reading and Writing

3 An **internal assessment** of Talk.

The **Folio** must be submitted to the Scottish Qualifications Authority (SQA) by the end of March of the year of the examination. It comprises:

– three **critical essays** (literature), from more than one genre

– two **writing pieces**: one **transactional** (discursive/argumentative/informational) essay, and one **personal/creative** essay.

The **examination** comprises:

– A **Writing paper**, 1 hour 15 minutes, covering a variety of topics. Candidates must produce an essay on one topic. The essay can be transactional, reflective or creative.

– Two **Close Reading** papers, 50 minutes each – in your case a General paper and a Credit paper.

Talk is assessed internally by your teacher.

How this book will help you

This book will take you through the course, helping you along the way. It is important throughout your Standard Grade course that you develop your reading, writing, and talking skills. It cannot be stressed strongly enough that these skills are not only related, they affect each other in a circular way. You become involved in an upward spiral: as you develop reading skills you become critically aware of techniques used by authors, techniques which you then adopt in your own writing thus improving your writing skills, all of which, in turn, sharpen your reading skills and so on…

It's the same with listening and talk. As you develop skills as a listener, you improve your own talk skills, which help make you aware of higher level listening skills and so on…

It all becomes a cycle of continuing development and skills improvement.

How this book will prepare you for the General and Credit award

The Standard Grade course extends over two years, but the most important year is the year leading up to the examination – usually your fourth year. This book concentrates on your fourth year work, including your preparation for your Folio. You will be studying a play, a novel, some short stories, maybe even some non-fiction, and, of course, a selection of poems. This book will help you enormously in showing you:

– how to study the literature

– how to prepare and write critical essays

– how to prepare effectively for the close reading papers.

But before we go any further, let's clear up a confusion. The term **reading** is used in Standard Grade to mean both **Close Reading** and **literature**. In this book we will avoid using the term **reading** unless when referring specifically to Standard Grade documents. Otherwise we will use the terms **Close Reading** and **literature**.

The skills that you need to develop

You will learn what is meant by the **theme** of a novel or play or poem. You will study the techniques by which authors portray or present their themes – techniques such as **structure**, **setting**, **characterisation**, **symbolism**. You will also learn about the importance of time in literature: the use of time as a structural device; the time when a book is written; the time period in which it is set; and the timescale over which it is written.

An essential part of your course is learning about **figures of speech**, terms such as **metaphor**, **simile**, **personification**, **alliteration**, **climax**. In poetry, you'll learn about **rhyme** and **rhythm** and **enjambement**. Sometimes these figures of speech are also known as **literary devices**. They are all part of the critical terminology that you will use in your critical essays.

! Look out for

You cannot tackle enough literature! It will develop your vocabulary immensely and give you confidence to approach most types of tasks and questions.

This book will help you learn all the things you need to know about language. You will find out about **sentence structure**, **lists**, **climactic sentences**, **link sentences**, **word choice** and **punctuation**. You will learn to recognise all the various question types in the Close Reading, so that you will be able to answer all the questions in the examination itself.

Writing skills

To gain the best marks, you need to develop various writing skills, such as how to write various kinds of essays: discursive, argumentative, personal/reflective, and how to compose a short story. You will learn how to introduce and structure your essays, including the critical essays that you produce for the Folio. The skills discussed in this book will help you write coherently and cohesively – with an introduction, paragraphs that are effectively linked, and a conclusion. You will also be shown how to draft and redraft your writing in order to improve its quality.

Talk skills

Finally, this book will help you develop your **Talk** skills. It is worth always bearing in mind that one third of your final grade is awarded for your performance in **Talk** – and that grade is assessed and awarded by your teacher. **Talk** involves your performance in groups and your performance solo. There is much you can do to improve your **Talk** skills, and that in turn will have quite an influence on your final overall grade.

But what is also important about this book is that not only will it help you prepare for and do well in Standard Grade, it will also help lay down the skills you need next year to do well in Higher English.

Recap

Now you know:

what Standard Grade involves

how this book will help you prepare for the assessments

how this book will help you attain a Credit award

how this book will also help you develop skills necessary for Higher.

The arrangements for your Standard Grade assessments

In Standard Grade, the word **assessment** covers that examination procedure, but it also covers the awarding of marks for procedures that are not part of a formal examination. For example, you are not examined in Talk but you are assessed and a grade is awarded. Similarly, the Folio submitted to the SQA is also an important part of your Standard Grade assessment but isn't an examination.

Standard Grade then involves procedures that are examination procedures and assessment procedures. The assessments are the Folio and Talk, the examination involves Close Reading papers and a Writing paper.

Look out for

Word processed Folio pieces are great, but be sure to proofread your pieces (don't just rely on your spellchecker!) and don't use crazy fonts!

Look out for

Be careful to ensure that your Folio pieces are of the correct length and not overly long!

Folio

The Folio is made up of **five pieces of work** produced by yourself throughout your Standard Grade course. You can choose any five pieces, but remember that you will have developed more skills and be more mature by the time you are in your fourth year, so it is sensible that you use work completed in your fourth year for your Folio.

We will look carefully in Chapters 6 and 7 at the kind of work you should produce for your Folio, but meantime let's be clear that you need to produce **five pieces of work comprising two writing pieces and three pieces of extended writing** (about 800 words if you are aiming for Credit) **on literary or media texts**.

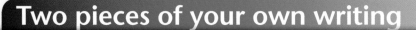

Two pieces of your own writing

The two pieces of your own writing must be:

▶ one of transactional / discursive kind that

　▶ conveys information; or

　▶ deploys ideas.

▶ one of expressive/imaginative kind that

　▶ describes personal experience, expressing feelings/emotions; or

　▶ employs a specific literary form, such as a short story/poem/letter.

Three critical essays on literary or media texts

Your critical essays should be:

▶ two critical essays from more than one genre (drama, prose, poetry); **and either**

▶ one critical essay from any one of these genres; **or**

▶ one critical essay of a media text (film, radio, television); **or**

▶ one imaginative response to a literary text or texts.

Look out for

Remember that printed material is no use if you want to tackle the media option!

The exam

The exam in May comprises two papers: the Close Reading paper and the Writing paper. You probably already know what is meant by an examination – you sit in a room full of other pupils, all of you in total silence, while the person in charge gives you paper (which will eventually be referred to as your exam 'script') and a question paper (referred to as your exam paper). You will then have to answer the questions posed by the paper in an allotted amount of time, at the end of which your script, along with everyone else's, will be gathered in and distributed to the appropriate teachers for marking.

Close Reading

Close Reading is assessed by the external examination in May. As far as you are concerned, there are two papers: General (which assesses grades 4 and 3) and Credit (which assesses grades 2 and 1). Each paper lasts 50 minutes, and the passages can be taken from fiction, journalism, or discursive material.

Writing

The exam also includes a Writing paper, which lasts for 1 hour 15 minutes. This paper is attempted by all candidates and will offer photographs as well as verbal stimuli. Your marks in this examination and your marks in the Writing pieces in your Folio will have equal weighting.

Talk assessment

Let's look at what the SQA's *Standard Grade Revised Arrangements in English* document says about Talk assessments:

For the purposes of assessment, Talking is regarded as falling within one or other of two categories, Discussion and Individual Talk. Discussion comprises all forms of talking in which the participants take turns to contribute; it includes, for example, reciprocal talk between individuals, interaction in groups, and contributions to discussion within the whole class. Individual Talk takes in all forms of talking in which the speaker communicates with minimum response on the part of the listener(s); the audience can range from a single listener to a group or class. It is recognised that these categories are not watertight and that activities such as interviews may legitimately be placed in either, according to whether or not the assignment calls for the participants to interact significantly.

If you want, you can undertake your Talk assessment with only your teacher present – and that might be better for those of you with a nervous disposition! Again, we are only looking at the business of assessment in this chapter – the details and advice will come later.

Grade Related Criteria

The other aspect of assessment that you need to know about and become familiar with are the Grade Related Criteria (GRC) which are used by the people who are employed by the SQA to mark your Folio and/or your external examinations (Writing and Close Reading). Each marker will use the relevant set of GRC to award your grade. Your teacher also has a copy of the GRC and will use them when setting your tasks and marking the work you do throughout the course. They can be found on the SQA website.

We will make reference to all the GRC (for Reading and Writing) throughout this book in order for you to understand all that is expected of you at Credit level.

How does the SQA arrive at your final grade?

Once your Folio has been externally assessed, the grades awarded to the Reading and Writing elements are matched with the grades awarded to your Close Reading papers and Writing papers to give an overall grade for Reading and Writing. If there is a significant difference between your performance in the examination and your Folio, everything is looked at again.

Your Talk grade has already been submitted by the school. All three grades (Reading, Writing, and Talk) are shown on your certificate.

Recap

Now you know:
- what is meant by the terms 'assessment' and 'examination'
- what is involved in the Folio
- what is involved in your Talk assessment
- what is involved in the Close Reading paper
- what is involved in the Writing paper
- what is meant by the Grade Related Criteria (GRC)
- how your final grades are decided.

The importance of language skills

Every aspect of Credit Standard Grade demands well-developed language skills. You already know that you have to be able to answer language questions in two Close Reading papers, but you also have to be able to write effectively and accurately (Folio and Writing paper) and you have to be able to analyse literature (Folio). All these tasks demand advanced skills in reading and writing.

Before we look at detailed Close Reading language questions, you need to know some grammar. Why? You might say that as a native English speaker, you already know as much as you need to know about grammar. You already read, write, speak, and listen to the language with a reasonable degree of fluency, so why do you need to know even more about the English language?

The obvious reason why you need to know some grammar is because such increased knowledge about language will increase your marks in the Close Reading, and that's a good enough reason.

What is grammar?

Grammar is the system of rules concerning the ways in which language is put together. Let's clarify the difference between **grammar** and **syntax**: **grammar** is the set of rules by which the entire **language** is put together, whereas **syntax** is the way in which an **individual sentence** has been constructed.

Word order

The way in which you arrange a sentence – any sentence – on a page is governed by the grammar of the language.

For example, you already know that it makes perfect sense to write:

The ship with the broken rudder sank in the harbour.

And that it makes little sense to write:

The sank harbour rudder ship the broken the in with.

You can see right away that the order in which we place the words in English is what determines sense. Meaning in an English sentence depends on word order and not really on word endings (unlike many other languages).

In English, you alter meaning when you rearrange the order of the words in a sentence – therefore knowing about rules which govern word order will help you in your reading and in your writing.

Let's look at some examples. Take the sentence:

The boy loves the girl.

Change the word order:

The girl loves the boy.

and you have changed the meaning. You can work out the difference!

Different types of sentences

There are five kinds of sentences:

▶ simple sentence

▶ compound sentence

▶ complex sentence

▶ compound-complex sentence

▶ minor sentence

The most basic kind of sentence is the **simple sentence**. It has only **one main verb**. For example, take the sentence:

The girl ate the apple.

First of all, we'll identify the **verb** in the sentence.

The verb

The **verb** is traditionally referred to as the 'doing word', and while that term is useful, it can be misleading.

In the sentence above the verb is quite definitely the doing word – what did the girl **do**? – she **ate** the apple!

But sometimes a verb does not signal action. Sometimes it signals a state of being or existence. Take the sentence:

My house stands at the edge of town.

Clearly, the house isn't **doing** anything – it is just standing there. But **stands** is still a verb. In the sentence **My hair is brown** the word **is** is still a verb – even although once again it isn't a 'doing word'.

We can have **verbs of action** and other verbs are more **verbs of being** (or **existing**) than doing. In almost all ways, the verb is the most important part of the sentence. Some sentences are verbless (but more of them later).

The subject

Let's go back to the first sentence we mentioned:

The girl ate the apple.

The verb is **ate**. If there is an answer to the question 'who ate?' or 'what ate?' then we have the **subject** of the sentence. The answer in this case is **The girl**.

We use the letter **V** to indicate the verb and the letter **S** to indicate the subject:

S	**V**	
The girl	ate	the apple

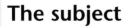

continued

Different types of sentences – continued

The object

With **verbs of action** (as opposed to **verbs of being**), such as **ate** and **shoot**, there is an **object** (**O**) if there is a recipient of that action. In the sentence, the apple is the recipient of the action **ate**, so the **apple** is the object:

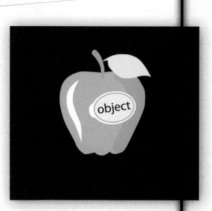

S	V	O
The girl	ate	the apple

Just as we ask of the verb 'who ate?' or 'what ate?', it can be useful to ask 'ate what?' or even 'ate whom?' – if there is an answer to such a question after a doing or action verb, then there is an object.

The complement

Things are slightly different if we are dealing with a **verb of being**. Let's take the sentence:

The sea is blue.

Here the word **blue** isn't the result of any action, but instead it says something about the subject, **the sea**: **blue** is an adjective describing **the sea** and therefore must agree with it. You will find out more about adjectives on page 20.

The word **blue** isn't the object of the verb since the verb **to be** isn't a verb of action – and so we call it the **complement** (**C**) because it 'completes' the subject, and it **must agree** with the **subject** (**S**) in number and gender.

Another example of the complement is:

S	V	C
The dog	is	clever

Now think about:

S	V	C
It	is	he

Or maybe you would prefer to say:

S	V	C
It	is	him

Remember what we said about the complement having to agree in **number** and **gender** with the subject? Which means that, technically, it is correct to say **It is he** since **him** is an object. When you think about it, most people would say **It is *he* who laughs last** and **It is *he* who hesitates who is lost.** To say, **It is *him* who laughs last** and **It is *him* who hesitates** sounds odd! Usage, however, has probably meant that most people would say **It is him** or **It's me** (rather than **It is I**) yet we would avoid *Him* **it is who has destroyed the castle. He it is who destroyed the castle** sounds better and is, in fact, more logical.

Different types of sentences – continued

The adjunct

Any other elements of the sentence, apart from the **verb**, the **subject**, and the **object** or **complement** are called the **adjunct** (**A**), because they **add** to the sentence. For example:

S	V	O	A
The girl	ate	the apple	slowly

or

S	V	O	A
The girl	ate	the apple	on the platform

or

S	V	O	A
The tram	is	stationary	at the terminus

Now that you know the labels for the various parts of a sentence (**subject, verb, object, complement, adjunct**) we can express normal sentence word order using these terms.

Look out for

Once you are aware of normal word order, it becomes much easier to describe any alteration to that order. We can now put the knowledge you have just gained to good use!

Normal sentence structure

The normal structure of a sentence in English is **S V O A** – subject, verb, object, adjunct – or **S V C A** – subject, verb, complement, adjunct.

Remember what we said about what happens if you alter word order – that is when you alter the position of any individual words? The same is true of the **structure** of a sentence. If you alter the structure of the sentence, the functions of the parts remain the same though the **meaning** is altered. An example will make all this clearer:

The girl ate the apple on the platform.

Now let's alter the structure by moving the adjunct to the beginning of the sentence:

A	S	V	O
On the platform,	the girl	ate	the apple

With the adjunct now at the beginning of the sentence, the word order is no longer in the normal **S V O A** order. Also, because the normal pattern has been broken, a comma is required after the adjunct. By placing the adjunct at the beginning of the sentence attention is drawn to it – we are drawing attention to *where* the girl ate the apple.

Other elements of normal sentences include **prepositions**, **adverbs**, **intensifiers**, **and sentence connectors** (sometimes referred to as sentence connectives).

Look out for

Whatever you have been taught about the use of the comma, it is important to know that commas are there for technical reasons, often to clarify meaning and avoid confusion. They are always needed whenever you move an adjunct to the beginning of a sentence. Commas are also used to separate items in a simple list.

Adverbs

Adverbs add meaning to or intensify the meaning of many other types of words – verbs, other adverbs, adjectives, prepositions, even an entire word group. For example:

- I wandered slowly — where **slowly** modifies the verb **wandered**

- I wandered very slowly — where **very** modifies another adverb **slowly**

- I wandered right over the ridge — where **right** modifies a prepositional phrase (which acts as another adverb)

- I wandered even when tired — where **even** intensifies the word group **when tired**

- You can define adverbs in terms of questions. For example, in the sentence **I am crossing the road** *now*, the adverb *now* answers the question **When are you crossing the road?** In this case, **now** is an adverb of time.

Adverbs – continued

Uses of adverbs

Adverbs can have a whole range of uses:

▶ **adverbs of time** answer the question 'when?' – before, afterwards, since, then, already, soon, now, indefinitely – as in **I am crossing the road** *now*. Have we met *before? Afterwards,* I want to go for a hamburger. I have postponed going abroad *indefinitely.*

▶ **adverbs of place** answer the question 'where?' – here, there, everywhere as in **I am** *at* **school**. My football is *nowhere* to be found. The plane is *on* the runway.

▶ **adverbs of manner** answer the question 'how?' – slowly, gradually, easily, swiftly, messily, badly, willingly, freely as in **I jumped the fence** *easily*. The man could see the other side of the river *clearly*. He went *willingly*. She received the gift *graciously*.

▶ **adverbs of degree** answer the question 'to what extent?' – quite, really, rather, almost, sufficiently as in **She is** *almost* **beautiful**. The dog is *quite* blind. The play was *rather* amusing. The tide is *sufficiently* out to use the causeway. She was *somewhat* amused.

▶ **adverbs of number** answer the question 'how often?' – once, twice, thrice as in **He painted the canvas** *twice***.**

▶ **adverbs which intensify (intensifiers)** answer the question 'how important?' or 'to what extent?' – very, even, extremely, too, also, certainly as in *Even* **he is able to understand adverbs.** *Only* she can train the dog. That river is *extremely* dangerous. Tom *also* can speak French.

▶ **adverbs of affirmation** answer the question 'how certain?' – yes, probably, possibly, maybe as in **I shall** *possibly* **go to the cinema tomorrow.** *Yes,* I am 16. *Surely* Joe will plant those trees?

▶ **adverbs of negation** answer the question 'how uncertain?' – not, no, unlikely, abnormally as in *No,* **I am not yet 16.** It is *unlikely* I shall go to the club.

▶ **sentence connectors**. Adverbs such as **nevertheless, moreover, additionally, however** and many others can be used as sentence connectors, which are not the same things as conjunctions. Many people mistakenly use **however** as a conjunction – which it is not. Therefore,

> **I tried to get £25 out of the machine, however there wasn't enough money in my account**

is quite definitely wrong. The adverb **however** connects the two sentences but it cannot join them. Therefore, the sentence should be

> **I tried to get £25 out of the machine; however, there wasn't enough money in my account**

where the semi-colon can splice the two parts of the sentence together, or you have to use an actual conjunction

> **I tried to get £25 out of the machine, but, however, there wasn't enough money in my account.**

Adverbs often appear at the beginning of sentences:

Occasionally, I go to the cinema.
Sometimes I go to the theatre.
From time to time, I enjoy reading a newspaper.

Look out for

Quite often, in Standard Grade Close Reading you are asked to comment on sentence structure, and the answer is made all the easier if you know about prepositional phrases and adverbs – and the effect of their position on meaning!

Adjectives

An adjective is a word which is used to describe or modify a noun. There are various kinds of adjectives:

▶ **descriptive adjectives** describe nouns: hard clean good ugly pretty young fluffy pendulous

▶ **colour adjectives** indicate colour: blue puce yellow green red

▶ **number adjectives** indicate anything to do with numbers and quantity: three both double many few some second fourth

▶ **demonstrative adjectives** refer to objects or people already mentioned – this that these those or to objects at a distance – yonder. They are also used to draw attention to a noun: for example, *These* berries are very ripe. *That* mountain is snow–clad. *This* path is very steep. *Those* cars are automatic.

▶ **interrogative adjectives** are used to ask questions – Which? Whose? What? as in *Whose* scarf is that? *Which* channel do you want to watch? *What* time is it?

▶ **determiner adjectives** enable the reader to determine aspects of the noun – the a each every either neither as in I am happy to watch *either* channel or *Each* apple has been hand-picked or The boy bought *a* ticket for the cinema.

▶ **comparative adjectives** are used when comparisons are made between **two** items or people (the comparative is formed either by adding *–er* to the adjective, when the adjective is short, or by using the word *more* before an adjective of three or more syllables) – Andrew is *taller* than Alison. Kevin is *more* sophisticated than Clark. That tree is the *taller* of the two.

▶ **superlative adjectives** are used in comparing **more than two items or people** (the superlative is formed either by adding *–est* to the adjective when it is short or by using the word *most* before an adjective of three or more syllables) – Alison is the *cleverest* of her friends. That tree is the *tallest* of the three. That sofa is the *most* comfortable of them all.

Sometimes, however, a different word is used for the comparative and the superlative:

good / better / best
many / more / most
little / less / least
much / more / most
bad / worse / worst

Prepositions

Prepositions indicate relationships between objects and/or people.

▶ Where is the dog? He is *under* the table. In relation to the table, the dog is *under* it.

▶ I see my therapist *on* Tuesday. The relationship between seeing the therapist and Tuesday is established by the preposition *on*.

In the first example, the preposition indicates place and in the second it indicates time.

Furthermore, **under the table** and **on Tuesday** are known as **prepositional phrases**. Prepositions (as the word implies) go **before** a noun or noun phrase (*On* the motorway, *in* the morning, *during* the news, *after* breakfast, *beyond* the junction, the person *in* whom you show such interest), though very often prepositional phrases have an adverbial function. But when the prepositional phrase comes after the noun it does not have an adverbial function.

In the sentence **I have a yellow SAAB with a black roof**, the prepositional phrase *with a black roof* does **not** have an adverbial function. It has an adjectival function as a post-modifier of a yellow SAAB.

Verb tenses

You already know how to identify a verb – **verbs of action** and **verbs of being**, such as the verbs *to have* or *to be*. But now you need to know about the **tense** of a verb. Tenses allow us to express events in time. As a native speaker, you can instantly tell, for example, the difference between **I lived in Kirkcaldy for a long time** and **I have lived in Kirkcaldy for a long time**, yet both verbs are in the past tense. What is the difference in meaning between **I shall be living in Kirkcaldy** and **I should have been living in Kirkcaldy**? And between **I live in St Andrews** and **I am living in St Andrews**? What are the differences in meaning of: **I shall live in Stornoway** and **I shall have been living in Stornoway** and **I should have been living in Stornoway**?

You need to know about tense since sometimes a Close Reading question demands knowledge of tense. For example, an author might switch from a past tense to the present tense for dramatic effect. If you know about tense, you can spot such a switch immediately.

There are many tenses in English but you should be able to recognise at least present, past, and future.

Present tense

In English, there are three present tenses, unlike many other languages which have only one. The table below sets out the **conjugation** of the three present tenses of the verb *to jump*. You should be able to work out the difference between the three present tenses.

Indefinite Present		
Person	**Singular**	**Plural**
First (I)	I jump	We jump
Second (you)	You jump	You jump
Third (he/she/it)	He/she/it jumps	They jump

Continuous Present		
Person	**Singular**	**Plural**
First (I)	I am jumping	We are jumping
Second (you)	You are jumping	You are jumping
Third (he/she/it)	He/she/it is jumping	They are jumping

Emphatic Present		
Person	**Singular**	**Plural**
First (I)	I do jump	We do jump
Second (you)	You do jump	You do jump
Third (he/she/it)	He/she/it does jump	They do jump

Past tense

The past tense is used for events that have happened in the past: the past indefinite, the past continuous, the past emphatic, the perfect indefinite, the perfect continuous, the past perfect indefinite and the past perfect continuous.

- past indefinite – I jumped
- past continuous – I was jumping
- past emphatic – I did jump

(The past continuous tense is sometimes referred to as the **imperfect tense**.)

There are also the perfect tense and the past perfect:

- perfect indefinite – I have jumped
- perfect continuous – I have been jumping
- past perfect indefinite – I had jumped
- past perfect continuous – I had been jumping

Future tense

The future tense is used for events that will happen in the future. Unlike some other languages (such as French), we cannot indicate the future by altering the ending of the verb (as we can when we form the past indefinite). We have to form the future tense by using an auxiliary verb such as *shall* or *will*.

▶ future indefinite – I shall jump

▶ future continuous – I shall be jumping

We can also use the present tense of *to go* to form the future, as in: I am going to the cinema tonight.

Knowledge of verb tense can help answer questions about sentence structure.

Auxiliary verbs

In the case of **I jump** we have the main verb itself. The past continuous tense of **I jump** is **I was jumping**. You note the word **was** (part of the verb **to be**) + the word **jumping**. In the perfect tense – **I have jumped** – there is the word **have** (part of the verb **to have**) + the main verb **jumped**.

Was and **have** (parts of the verbs **to be** and **to have**) are referred to as **auxiliary verbs**: they help convey the meaning of the verb. For example, **I shall jump** indicates the future and **I might be jumping** is a conditional tense (since some condition has to be met before I do the jumping).

Finite and non-finite verbs

There are two parts to each verb: the **finite** and the **non-finite**. The non-finite part of the verb is perhaps easier to deal with first. The non-finite part is the infinitive of the verb (to jump, to run, to drink, to be, to have, to snigger) and any incomplete part of a verb such as eating, going, broken, dropped.

A finite verb is then any **main verb**.

An example will make things clearer:

I walked down the road eating an apple

There is only one main verb in that sentence: **walked** – that then is the **finite** verb. Because **eating** is only a part of the verb, it is known as a **non-finite** verb. Therefore **I walked down the road eating an apple** is a simple sentence – it has only one clause – analysed thus:

S	V	A	A
I	walked	down the road	eating an apple

The **finite** verb is the main verb, and, as such, defines a clause. The **non-finite** verb forms an adjunct.

Let's try another one. Take the sentence:

Smothering the flames with a blanket, the air hostess managed to extinguish the fire.

Here the main verb is **managed**. The other verbs are non-finite: **Smothering** and **to extinguish**. Therefore the analysis is as follows:

A	S	V	O
Smothering the flames with a blanket,	the air hostess	managed	to extinguish the fire

Main and subordinate clauses

Now you need to know about **clauses**. A clause is a group of words with a **finite verb**. There are two clauses: the **Main Clause** and **Subordinate Clauses**. Once you can identify these, it becomes much easier to describe the difference between formal and informal English.

The **main clause** is independent and makes sense by itself, whereas the **subordinate clause** is subordinate to the main clause and does not make sense on its own.

For example, we set the analysis out as shown below, using parallel vertical lines to indicate the boundaries between the clauses:

MC		**SC**
I knocked on the classroom door		so that the teacher would hear me.

In this sentence, the clause **I knocked on the classroom door** can stand by itself and make sense, therefore it is the **main clause**. The clause **so that the teacher would hear me** cannot stand by itself and make sense, therefore it is the subordinate clause.

In this next example, the subordinate clause comes before the main clause:

SC		**MC**
Before we deal with the various kinds of sentences,		you need to know about clauses.

The clause **you need to know about clauses** can stand alone and make sense, therefore it is the **main clause**, and obviously **Before we deal with the various kinds of sentences** is dependent on or subordinate to it.

Let's look at another example:

The girl ate the apple on the platform, before she boarded the train.

Which is the main clause? It is fairly obvious that **before she boarded the train** cannot stand alone and make complete sense: it depends on the other clause for context. **The girl ate the apple on the platform** is the **main clause** and **before she boarded the train** is the **subordinate clause**.

MC		**SC**
The girl ate the apple on the platform,		before she boarded the train.

Subordination

Subordination can be defined as shifting the subordinate clause to the beginning of the sentence. This can have the effect of drawing attention to its meaning or of creating climax by delaying the main point to the end of the sentence. The use of subordination can also give your writing style some variety, thus making it more interesting for the reader. The use of subordination also tends to make writing more formal.

Look at this example:

| **SC** | | | | **MC** |
| Although I like maths, | | | | I really prefer English. |

What is the effect of placing the subordinate clause at the beginning of the above sentence? It draws attention to the clause – one of concession concerning maths – while making the preference for English clear by placing it climactically at the end of the sentence.

Complex sentences

A **complex sentence** is one where there is one main clause and one or more subordinate clauses, as in all the above examples, and in the following one:

| **MC** | | | | **SC** |
| Lennie crawled slowly and cautiously around the fire | | | | until he was close to George. |

Compound sentences

A **compound sentence** is where there are **two main clauses** and no subordinate clauses. The two clauses are often connected by a conjunction.

For example:

| **MC** | | | **MC** |
| The boy knocked on the classroom door, | | | **and** the teacher told him to come in. |

or

| **MC** | | | **MC** |
| The boy knocked on the classroom door, | | | **and** went straight in. |

In the above example, the subject of **went straight in** is the boy, and you note that **straight** in this sentence is an adverb – it tells you *how* the boy went in.

or

| **MC** | | | **MC** |
| We could go shopping this afternoon, | | | **or else** we could go to the cinema. |

Look out for

Note that because the verb **could go** in the second clause has a subject **we**, then a comma before the conjunction is technically necessary.

Compound-complex sentences

A sentence with two or more main clauses and one or more subordinate clauses is called a **compound-complex sentence**, and is invariably found in formal prose.

For example:

MC		**MC**
I knocked on the classroom door,		**and** the teacher told me to come in,

SC	**MC**	**SC**
but when she saw me,	she gave me a row,	because I had not finished my essay.

The minor sentence

A minor sentence is a sentence without a verb or without a finite verb. Look at the following extract from George Orwell's *Marrakech*:

As they went past a tall, very young Negro turned and caught my eye. But the look he gave me was not in the least the kind of look you might expect. Not hostile, not contemptuous, not sullen, not even inquisitive. It was the shy, wide-eyed Negro look, which actually is a look of profound respect.

Read carefully the third sentence: **Not hostile, not contemptuous, not sullen, not even inquisitive.** You'll notice that there is no verb in this sentence, therefore it is a **minor sentence**. Knowing that it is a minor sentence is not enough – you also have to be able to comment on the effect. You'll also notice that it is structured as a list and that there are no conjunctions: a list with no conjunctions is called an **asyndetic list** (see below) and the technique is known as **asyndeton**.

A minor sentence is usually effective because it creates impact. Drama, even! (Did you note that minor sentence?) They are especially effective when the minor sentence is a one word sentence, even a one-word paragraph, as is sometimes the case.

The asyndetic list is effective often because it is, as in the example from the Orwell extract, climactic in structure. Notice that in the sentence **Not hostile, not contemptuous, not sullen, not even inquisitive**, the word **even** has an adverbial function, acting as an intensifier, stressing that the look given by the boy was not in any sense unpleasant. The adjectives become less and less aggressive, suggesting, climactically, that the boy was no threat to the white men present.

Lists and their effects

It is important to understand that there are three types of lists and that they can be used for different purposes.

Polysyndetic lists, where there are conjunctions between each item. The effect is usually to stress that each item carries equal importance. It can also give the impression that the items are significantly and causally linked and/or to create a cumulative effect.

Asyndetic lists, where there are no conjunctions between each item. The effect is usually to:

▶ suggest range and/or extent and/or variety of whatever is being discussed

▶ create climax.

Lists in parallel structure, where the structural pattern of each item is repeated. For example, the pattern could be a verb in the infinitive followed by a prepositional phrase:

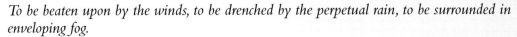
> *To be beaten upon by the winds, to be drenched by the perpetual rain, to be surrounded in enveloping fog.*
>
> The effect is often climactic (working up to a main point) or it may be again to stress the range and extent of whatever is being discussed.

Literary devices

Literary devices are ways of writing which can help make writing more interesting and more effective. Good writers will use a wide range of literary devices. For Standard Grade, you need to know about:

- metaphor and simile
- onomatopoeia
- alliteration
- hyperbole
- personification.

Metaphor and simile

Metaphor and simile are devices of comparison. With **metaphor**, one thing is said to **be another** or described in terms of another. With **simile** one thing is said to be **like another**.

Let's deal with metaphor first of all. The following are two lines from a poem *To His Coy Mistress* by Andrew Marvell. In it, the persona (the person narrating the poem) bemoans the fact that life is so short, that time flies so quickly. He wants, if he could have it, centuries of time to adore his mistress but, he says, 'Time' is at his back 'hurrying near':

> *But at my back I always hear*
> *Time's wingèd Chariot hurrying near:*

You have heard about 'analysing' an image, but sometimes we talk about 'deconstructing' an image, by which we mean undoing the image to explain, in the first instance, the literal meaning of the image, and then to examine how the writer applies it figuratively – i.e., metaphorically.

In the lines above, time is being compared to a wingèd Chariot. We must first of all deconstruct the image. What is a chariot? It was a two-wheeled horse-drawn carriage, driven at speed (and often quite brutally) in races. When Marvell adds the adjective **wingèd**, he adds to the impression of swiftness and speed. He is comparing the idea of time passing with the idea of Time driving a fast chariot.

It's useful to set out – step by step – the process that you should follow (though in the actual examination you do not need to set out the following steps). As we have already said, metaphor involves a comparison – but you have to be careful because the comparison may not always be obvious. Metaphors can lurk unseen in the shadows!

Let's refer to the thing being compared (in this case **Time**) as **Term A** and the thing it is being compared to (in this case a **wingèd chariot**) we'll call **Term B**. We can set it out thus:

Time's wingèd Chariot hurrying near

Term A   Term B

Now you have to go to Term B and state the literal meaning:

Time's wingèd Chariot hurrying near

Term A   Term B

two-wheeled horse-drawn carriage, small,
light, fast, seatless, used for chariot racing.

Marvell is then comparing Time (that is, the passage of time), to a racing chariot, making the
point that Time speeds on, just like a chariot in a race. Time is very swift and comes hurrying
after us, as in a race.

Onomatopoeia

Onomatopoeia is the use of words which sound like the sounds they describe. Read the
following lines:

*I am now primed. My heart is thumping against my ribs, one by one, like a hammer
pounding out a musical scale on a metal keyboard. Bing. Bang. Bong. Bam. I am breathing so
quickly that I cannot breathe, if that makes any sense.*
I am aware of every single one of my classmates in Maths.
*Everyone in Maths is now preoccupied. There are only four minutes left in the period. Mrs
Moonface is filling up blackboard space at an unprecedented speed, no doubt trying to scrape
every last kernel of mathematical knowledge from the corncob of her brain before the bell. My
classmates are racing to keep up with her. All around me pens are moving across notebooks at
such a rate that ink can barely leak out and affix itself to paper.*
*My moment is at hand! The great clapper in the bell of fate clangs for me! Ka-wang! Ka-
wang!*

In the example above, the words 'Bing. Bang. Bong. Bam.' attempt to imitate the actual
sound, supposedly of his heart pounding on the keyboard. There are other onomatopoeic
words: 'Ka-wang! Ka-wang!' The effect of the onomatopoeic words is to draw attention to
the sounds, and in this case, to suggest John's growing excitement. The very vowel sounds
'Bing. Bang. Bong. Bam.' suggest an increasing noise, culminating in the final 'Bam'.
The increasing noise suggests his increasingly loud heartbeat and therefore his increasing
excitement.

The other example of onomatopoeia, 'Ka-wang! Ka-wang!', is used to capture the noise of
the bell – and he says that it's 'the bell of fate' that 'clangs' (more onomatopoeia) for him. In
this sentence, we have a metaphor – the school bell is the bell of fate – and onomatopoeia.

Alliteration

The example above has an example of alliteration, in which the same initial letter is repeated in a number of successive words. The repetition of the **B** sound in the words 'Bing. Bang. Bong. Bam.' draws attention to the letter **B**, which is the most violent, explosive, noisy letter in our alphabet. This means that it can be used to express anger or noise. Here it is used to express increasing noise and therefore increasing excitement.

Hyperbole

Hyperbole is the term used when descriptions are exaggerated. The excerpt on page 26, has a number of examples:

Mrs Moonface is filling up blackboard space at an unprecedented speed.
The great clapper in the bell of fate clangs for me.
…pens are moving across notebooks at such a rate that ink can barely leak out and affix itself to paper.

The use of hyperbole here contributes to the suggestion of the narrator's growing excitement.

Personification

Personification is the name we give to the device by which we attribute human (or animal) characteristics to inanimate objects. Look at the following sentence: Within minutes we were at Gizeh – the ruins **overwhelmed** by the traffic and the bright lights, the tenements and bazaar; The word **overwhelmed** means to be overcome by emotions or to be overcome physically or to be submerged by something. The writer is stating that the ruins are being overcome by the bright lights – in other words, a human characteristic is being attributed to the ruins.

Punctuation

You already know the basic elements of punctuation, but you should also know that punctuation marks can have a variety of roles and can be important tools in your writing. You need to know about:

▶ the colon

▶ the semi-colon

▶ the single dash

▶ the paired comma (and the paired dash and brackets)

▶ inverted commas

The colon

The colon has four main uses:

▶ **To introduce or indicate a list**. The colon has always been used to introduce lists, but the dash is gradually replacing it. In formal prose, however, it is usual to use the colon rather than the dash.

Look at Philip Larkin's use of the colon in the following sentence from the first stanza of *Church Going*:

Another church: matting, seats, and stone,
And little books; sprawlings of flowers, cut
For Sunday, brownish now; some brass and stuff
Up at the holy end; the small neat organ;
And a tense, musty, unignorable silence,
Brewed God knows how long.

The colon after church introduces the list of everything that the persona sees inside this particular church that he is visiting.

▶ **To signal an explanation following a statement**. The colon has traditionally been used to signal an explanation of a statement, but is gradually being replaced by the dash. In formal prose, however, it is usual to use the colon rather than the dash. For example:

And yet the dodo is more than a cheap laugh: the dodo is an icon.

In this sentence the colon signals the explanation as to why the dodo is more than just a laugh: it is an icon, a symbol of something much more important than a cause for laughter.

▶ **To indicate balance in a sentence**. This is a very formal use of the colon and suggests an almost poetic tone. The most famous example is To err is human: to forgive divine.

▶ **To introduce or signal a quotation.**

The semi-colon

The semi-colon is a much underused and underrated punctuation mark. It is actually extremely useful, and you should attempt to use it in your own writing.

> ▶ **To indicate a connection between two independent but related units of sense**. A common error nowadays is what we call **the comma splice**, where a comma is used to join together (or splice) two units of sense that are clearly related but which are syntactically independent.

For example, in the sentence:

My dad bought me a dog, however he says I have to walk and feed it myself.

the comma is not strong enough to join the two clauses. Also, remember what we said about the word **however**: it is not a conjunction. Although it is a sentence connector, it cannot actually join two units of sense into one sentence – neither can the comma. The simplest way to remedy this problem is to substitute a semi-colon for the comma:

My dad bought me a dog; however he says I have to walk and feed it myself.

It could, of course, be made into two separate sentences:

My dad bought me a dog. However he says I have to walk and feed it myself.

There is, however, a useful guideline for stylish writing which suggests that **however** should be placed as closely as possible to the beginning of a sentence but **never** the first word. Thus, the following is more appealing:

My dad bought me a dog. He says, however, I have to walk and feed it myself.

Finally, the two could be linked by a relative pronoun:

My dad bought me a dog, which he says I have to walk and feed myself.

But by far the most effective way of joining these two units is by the semi-colon. And its use adds style to your writing.

> ▶ **To separate complex items in a list where commas are already used**. For example:

There is no doubt that obesity is the world's biggest public-health issue today – the main cause of heart disease, which kills more people these days than AIDS, malaria, war; the principal risk factor in diabetes; heavily implicated in cancer and other diseases.

There are three items in the list:

1 the main cause of heart disease, which kills more people these days than AIDS, malaria, war;

2 the principal risk factor in diabetes;

3 heavily implicated in cancer and other diseases.

You'll notice that the first item itself contains a list: **which kills more people these days than AIDS, malaria, war**, and you also notice that the items within this list are separated by commas, therefore to mark the end of this list and the end of item 2 the author has, quite rightly, used semi-colons – thus avoiding any confusion.

The single dash

The single dash has several functions. Sometimes the single dash is used to introduce an afterthought, but in many cases nowadays the single dash is replacing the colon in function. Let's look at various uses of the single dash:

▶ **To signal an explanation following a statement**. For example, in the sentence:

For more than a century scientists had assumed that the Dodo's ancestors must have reached Mauritius from Africa – because this is the nearest continental land mass.

The dash after Africa signals that an explanation for the scientists' assumptions is to follow.

▶ **To indicate or introduce a list**, as in this sentence:

In fact, the name dodo didn't stick until other names had been tried – 'Kermis' after a Dutch annual fair, then 'walghvogel' which means 'nauseating fowl'.

The dash here introduces or signals the list of previous names for the dodo.

▶ **To indicate an afterthought**. This is the traditional use of the dash: My brother lost his job today – or was it yesterday?

Paired punctuation marks for parenthesis

Punctuation marks are often used in pairs, such as commas, dashes and brackets to indicate **parenthesis**. This device isolates additional information which is – and this is the important point – optional. It is not connected syntactically with the rest of the sentence. In other words, if you omit the parenthetical information, you do not affect the syntactic structure of the sentence. For example:

Luke went to the cinema – the one in Dunfermline – to see the latest Bond film.

The parenthesis, indicated in this case by the paired dash, is additional, optional information. It can be removed without affecting the syntax of the sentence – *Luke went to the cinema to see the latest Bond film.*

(You should also know that the plural of **parenthesis** is **parentheses**.)

The paired comma

Paired commas have two other uses, as well as signalling parenthesis. Paired commas can signal **vocative of address** or **apposition**:

▶ **Vocative of address**. We use paired commas round someone's name when we are actually addressing that person. For example, what is the difference between these two sentences?

We have met Gatsby, haven't we?

and

We have met, Gatsby, haven't we?

You see how punctuation is essential in clarifying meaning!

▶ **Apposition** Apposition, unlike parenthesis, is where the additional information, usually a noun phrase placed after a noun, is part of the syntax of the sentence and does modify meaning. For example:

Scott Fitzgerald, the author of The Great Gatsby, is the man who invented the term The Jazz Age.

The phrase **the author of *The Great Gatsby*** is obviously additional material **but** it modifies the meaning of Scott Fitzgerald in that it informs the reader of which Scott Fitzgerald we are talking about – the one who is the author of The Great Gatsby. That phrase is said to be in **apposition** to Scott Fitzgerald.

Look at this other example, from a letter to parents about arrangements on a school trip:

Your child will be travelling to Stratford-upon-Avon by coach and will be accompanied by Mr Keats, the head of the English Department, and his two departmental colleagues, Miss Orwell and Mrs Stoker.

In this case there are two noun phrases in apposition: **the head of the English Department** in apposition to **Mr Keats** and **Miss Orwell and Mrs Stoker**, in apposition to **his two departmental colleagues**. Apposition is actually a way of communicating and clarifying information effectively and concisely.

Inverted commas

Inverted commas are used for several purposes.

▶ **To indicate direct speech**. In the following example:

But the proclivities of those contestants and their parents in no way represent the general participant. "It's not just the geeks and the nerds. These are normal kids," says Ohio's Beth Richards, whose daughter, Bailey, was making her second appearance in the finals.

The words "**It's not just the geeks and the nerds. These are normal kids,**" are enclosed in inverted commas because these are the actual words spoken by Beth Richards.

▶ **To indicate the words of a quotation**. 'Life's but a walking shadow' (Macbeth)

Look out for

A hero who gives his/her name to the title is referred to as an 'eponymous hero'.

▶ **To indicate the title of books, plays, poems, film, television programmes**. For example: 'Macbeth'; 'In the Snack Bar'. It is important to indicate titles by the use of inverted commas (or by Italics if you are using a word processor) simply because the inverted commas signal that you are talking about the play Macbeth and not the character. The same is true of 'Hamlet' or 'Othello' or any work of literature where the piece takes its name from one of the characters.

▶ **To indicate a word used ironically or unusually or out of context**. In this extract, Karen Hicks tells reporter John Harlow about her celebrity worship:

She has fixed her sights on a new star: David Sneddon, winner of the television show Fame Academy. Last week she cornered Sneddon at two television appearances, though it is early days in her "acquaintance" with him. Yet she felt impelled to defend him indignantly against a TV presenter who, she thought, had not shown Sneddon sufficient respect.
Hicks is no deluded young teen: she is a 28-year-old electrical engineer. But she freely admits to an "addiction" to the latest musical sensations.

The use of inverted commas around the word "acquaintance" signals to the reader that the author is using Karen Hicks's word and is indicating, by the inverted commas, that it is being used ironically by him. He recognises that Karen Hicks is not acquainted (in the true meaning of the word) with David Sneddon nor is she likely to be.

On the other hand, in the second paragraph the inverted commas round the word "addiction" indicate that the word is being used in an unusual sense: Karen's obsession with musical sensations cannot be considered to be an addiction in the way in which, say, an alcoholic suffers from addiction.

Let's quickly recap

You now know:

- the five kinds of sentences: simple, compound, complex, compound-complex, and minor
- the functions in a simple sentence of the subject, the verb, the object and/or the complement, the adjunct
- the effect of moving the adjunct
- the function of an adverb and adverbial phrases
- the functions of tense in English
- the functions of auxiliary verbs
- the difference between finite and non-finite verbs
- the functions of the main and subordinate clauses
- the different types of lists
- the different functions for punctuation marks.

Thinking your way around the paper

There are about 25 or more questions asked in each of the General and Credit Close Reading papers (some 50 questions altogether). These can be reduced to many fewer question types. It is important that you are able to recognise the question types. This makes it much easier to answer the questions. The question type becomes a kind of template for you. It means you then can:

▶ instantly identify each question by its type

▶ check it mentally against the template

▶ know then exactly how to answer it.

In this chapter, we will examine in turn each question type by:

▶ giving you an example of the type

▶ showing you how to arrive at the answer

▶ giving you an example to try for yourself.

Look out for

In the actual exam, obviously you don't always have to show how you arrive at the answers – you only have to write down the answer!

We will not just give you the answer, since that isn't really very helpful. You will be shown **how** the answer is arrived at. You need to know how we have arrived at the answer, therefore you will get a step-by-step explanation.

And another thing: because the Close Reading paper is not a test of your writing skills, you do not have to write in sentences. Answers in note form are perfectly acceptable as long as you make the point(s) required.

Question types

An analysis of recent General and Credit Close Readings reveals that the most commonly asked question types are:

▶ questions about the meanings of ideas

▶ questions which demand evidence from the text

▶ questions about word choice and connotations of words

▶ questions about the meaning of an individual word or expression, though sometimes you are also asked to identify the context and show how it helps you arrive at the meaning.

There are other question types that appear less often:

▶ questions about sentence structure (including link sentences)

▶ questions about figures of speech

▶ questions about writer technique

▶ questions about punctuation

▶ questions about tone

▶ questions about the appropriateness of the title

▶ questions about conclusions.

Some of these questions take different forms, as you'll see as we deal with each in turn.

In the first example overleaf, you have to get the whole answer correct – usually they are looking for only one point but it has to be the right point in order to get the full 2 marks. In the second example, the 2|1|0 means that they are looking for two points, and if you only get one right you get 1 mark. If there are three points being asked for, you will get 2 marks for all three, 1 mark for only two correct points, and 0 for only one correct answer.

Questions about the meaning of ideas

Look out for

In recent Credit papers about one third of the questions have been about meanings of ideas. It is really vitally important that you answer in your own words.

Questions about the meaning of ideas are very common and you have to use your own words in your response. The best technique is to be clear about what the question is asking, then go to the passage to identify the answer.

Credit question 1 (2005)

Read the following opening paragraph:

> 1   Rameses 1 Station, usually called Cairo Railway Station, is a century old, like the railway system itself, which stretches from Alexandria on the shores of the Mediterranean, to Aswan on the Upper Nile, at the northern edge of lake Nasser – the border of Sudan on the south side. The design of the station is of interest, and it has been said that it represents the epitome of nineteenth-century Egyptian architects' desire to combine classical and Islamic building styles, in response to Khedive Ismail's plan to create a "European Cairo" – Moorish meets modern.

Look out for

Easy? The secret is to identify where in the passage the answer lies and then put it into your own words, without struggling to translate every word.

In your own words, what do Rameses I Station and the railway system have in common? [2|_|0]

Both are 100 years old.

The number 1 at the start of the paragraph refers to the paragraph number. This is useful because questions refer to specific numbered paragraphs. You then know precisely where the answer lies.

The marks ascribed are 2 or 0, which means the marker is looking for two points for a completely correct answer.

The first thing is to identify the answer in the text. Once you identify the relevant section in the text, it is a good idea to underline it: that is the section you are going to have to put into your own words. Remember that the exam paper belongs to you, therefore you can scribble helpful notes on it.

In the above example, the following is the relevant section:

Rameses I Station ..., **like the railway system itself**, is a century old.

The comparison like the railway system itself tells us that both the station and the railways themselves are a century old. But remember the answer must be given in your own words. (The three dots ... are called **ellipsis** and indicate that words have been omitted.)

Credit question 2 (2005)

Read the following paragraph:

2   Kings, queens, princes, heads of state and generals have arrived and departed here. One of Naguib Mahfouz's earliest heroes, the ultra-nationalist anti-British rabble rouser, Saad Zaghul, escaped an assassination attempt at Cairo Station on his return from one of his numerous exiles, in 1924. Given Egypt's history of dramatic arrivals and departures the railway figures as a focal point and a scene of many riotous send-offs and welcomes.

3   The best story about Cairo Railway Station, told to me by a man who witnessed it unfold, does not concern a luminary but rather a person delayed in the third class ticket queue. When this fussed and furious man at last got to the window he expressed his exasperation to the clerk, saying, "Do you know who I am?"

4   The clerk looked him up and down and, without missing a beat, said, "In that shabby suit, with a watermelon under your arm, and a Third Class ticket to El Minya, who could you possibly be?"

Look at Paragraphs 3 and 4. In your own words, explain what is surprising about the best story the writer has heard about Cairo Railway Station. [2|1|0]

It was surprising because it was not about anyone important – it was about an ordinary individual.

You'll notice that the question refers you to Paragraphs 3 and 4, but that Paragraph 2 has also been included. In order to answer this question accurately you have to realise that the station had witnessed many important people leave and depart, and that there was a history of dramatic arrivals and departures, with scenes of many riotous send-offs and welcomes. The writer then states that the best story … **does not concern a luminary but rather a person delayed in the third class ticket queue.** Therefore, the answer to what was the best story has to be the one that does not concern a luminary.

In a sense, the question is there to ascertain whether or not you know the meaning of the word **luminary**. The association of the man with the third class ticket queue should help you work it out. You will come across occasions when you won't be able to put some word into your own language – and you have to accept that. For example, there aren't really alternatives for terms such as 'railway station' or 'ticket': it's the gist of the piece of text that has to be in your own words.

Credit question 3 (2001)

Read the following paragraph carefully:

> 1   They didn't come to England till 1962. It was the "n"-th year of preparations for a visit that always, in the end, failed to happen.
> 2   I'd just arrived home for autumn half-term and at first I didn't believe what I was told – that their plane had touched down at the airport – and I wasn't convinced till I saw for myself the black Hawker Humber taxi come swinging up the drive, axles creaking, carrying its two passengers in the back, one swathed in furs.

The answer lies in the expressions It was the "n"-th year of preparations *and a* visit that always, in the end, failed to happen. *The skill, as always with these kind of questions, is putting it into your own words.*

In your own words, explain fully why the narrator at first didn't believe that 'their plane had touched down at the airport'. [2|1|0]

> Since they had got ready countless times for visits that were always cancelled at the last minute, the writer didn't believe this one would take place.

Credit question 4 (2008)

Read the following paragraph carefully:

> 1   The play—for which Briony had designed the posters, programmes and tickets, constructed the sales booth out of a folding screen tipped on its side, and lined the collection box in red crêpe paper—was written by her in a two-day tempest of composition, causing her to miss a breakfast and a lunch. When the preparations were complete, she had nothing to do but contemplate her finished draft and wait for the appearance of her cousins from the distant north. There would be time for only one day of rehearsal before her brother, Leon, arrived.
> 2   At some moments chilling, at others desperately sad, the play told a tale of the heart whose message, conveyed in a rhyming prologue, was that love which did not build a foundation on good sense was doomed. The reckless passion of the heroine, Arabella, for a wicked foreign count is punished by ill fortune when she contracts cholera during an impetuous dash towards a seaside town with her intended. Deserted by him and nearly everybody else, bed-bound in an attic, she discovers in herself a sense of humour. Fortune presents her a second chance in the form of an impoverished doctor—in fact, a prince in disguise who has elected to work among the needy. Healed by him, Arabella chooses wisely this time, and is rewarded by reconciliation with her family and a wedding with the medical prince on "a windy sunlit day in spring".

The marks ascribed are 2 or 0, which means the marker is looking for one correct answer. Clearly, however, there are two possible answers both of which have to be right:

Look at Paragraph 1.

What task has Briony been involved in? [2|_|0]

> Briony has been involved in writing a play
>
> **or**
>
> she has been involved in preparing for a performance of the play.

Either answer is correct.

Credit question 5 (2008)

Look now at Paragraph 2 in question 4 above.

Briony's play is a story with a message.

In your own words, explain what the message is. [2|1|0]

> Any love relationship based thoughtlessly on powerful emotion alone will inevitably end in misfortune.

Now try this

Credit question 6 (2006)

Read carefully the following paragraph:

> Though it might seem arcane in the age of computer spellcheck programs, more than nine million American children took part in spelling contests this year, with the top 265 progressing to Washington for the grand finals last week.

Explain **in your own words** why spelling contests might seem 'arcane' or strange. [2|1|0]

Credit question 7 (2001)

Read carefully the following paragraph:

> 18 I examined my cousin surreptitiously while I helped my father carry the cases to the foot of the staircase – while he just stood there, doing nothing. He was odd-looking, I saw. He had a triangular-shaped face with a bony chin, and he was bloodlessly, alarmingly pale. He stood with his shoulders hunched; very arched eyebrows and flat ears set close against his head added to the pixie-ness of his appearance. What made me think him odder still was his not seeming to match at all with his elegant (and from what I could see, pretty) mother. (How ugly must his father be, I wondered, to correct the balance of heredity?) He was several inches shorter than I was, although I knew we were the same age (eleven, if the year was 1962). His height – or his lack of height – was another disappointment, and also his thinness. I'd expected he would look stolid, and assertive, and the very picture of glowing health. Instead the eyes in his pale face flitted among us, like a prying spinster's, missing nothing.

'He was odd-looking…' Explain in your own words what the narrator seemed to think was the strangest thing about his cousin. [2|_|0]

Remember to look at the text and decide which sentences contain the answer. Part of the answer has to be in the first sentence: a tale of the heart … (which conveys) that love which did not build a foundation on good sense was doomed.

But the marks depend on your using your own words, which could be: love / relationships based solely on passion will end in disaster.

Then there is the following in the second sentence: The reckless passion of the heroine… is punished by ill fortune *could be answered as: thoughtlessness ends in disaster / misery / ruin / tragedy / catastrophe / misfortune.*

Look out for

Remember, if you don't use your own words you won't score any marks.

Questions which demand evidence from the text

Questions which demand evidence from the text are very common in both the General and Credit Close Reading papers. In recent Credit and General Close Reading papers, about one third of questions involved gathering evidence from the text. It is important that you know how to recognise such questions and how to answer them.

The following question is adapted from a recent Credit Close Reading paper. It is about a writer's visit to Maes Howe, one of the most important archaeological sites in Orkney.

Credit question 8 (2007)

Read carefully Paragraphs 9 to 14:

> 9 Alan, an Englishman in Historic Scotland tartan trousers, led me into a little shop to issue a ticket. The shop was housed in an old water mill, some distance from the tomb, and sold guidebooks and fridge magnets and tea towels. From the window you could see over the main road to the tomb.
> 10 "Tell you what," he said. "I'll give you a ticket so you can come back tomorrow, if you like, but I can't give you one for the actual solstice, Saturday. We start selling them at two-thirty on the actual solstice. It's first come, first served."
> 11 "How many people come?"
> 12 "Well, we can accommodate 25, at a pinch."
> 13 But today there was only myself.
> 14 The young guide, Rob, was waiting outside.

When you are asked for **three** of anything, remember that you must provide all three to get the 2 marks available. Any two would be worth 1 mark, and, obviously, if you only provide 1 you get zero marks.

Look at Paragraph 9 – what evidence is there that the place is like any other tourist attraction? Go through the paragraphs methodically:
(a) the person in charge is wearing Historic Scotland tartan trousers, (i.e. a uniform)
(b) it has a shop
(c) it issues tickets
(d) sells guidebooks
(e) sells fridge magnets
(f) sells tea towels
(g) there is a guide.
Now choose any three of the above for full marks!

Give **three** pieces of evidence which suggest that Maes Howe is just like any other tourist attraction. [2|1|0]

Maes Howe is like any other tourist attraction because it has a shop, it issues tickets and sells guidebooks.

General question 1 (2007)

Read the following paragraphs:

Biker Boys and Girls

There is only one "wall of death" doing the rounds at British fairs today. But a new generation of daredevil riders is intent on keeping the show on (or rather, off) the road.

1   Last year Kerri Cameron, aged 19 and a little bored with her job as a horse-riding instructor, was looking up job vacancies on the internet. Puzzled, she turned to her mother and said, "Mum, what's a wall of death?"

2   Her mother, Denise, a health worker who has always had a horror of motorcycles, told her that walls of death were places where people rode motorbikes round the insides of a 20 ft-high wooden drum and tried not to fall off and get killed. "Gosh," said Kerri, "that sounds fun."

3   She picked up her mobile, phoned the number mentioned on the internet and then arranged to see Ken Fox, owner of the wall of death. Ken Fox didn't ask about her school qualifications, only if she wanted a ride on the back of his bike around the wall. Yes, she said.

Look at Paragraph 2. Be careful because the question is not just about Kerri's reaction but is about the surprising nature of her reaction. The surprise is that she thinks that motorcyclists trying to avoid being killed sounds like fun. Do you see, though, that you are still going to the text for evidence? You need to make reference to the text to get the right answer.

What is surprising about Kerri's reaction to what her mother tells her about the wall of death? [2|1|0]

General question 2 (2007)

Read the following paragraphs:

11 The first wall of death is said by Graham Cripsey to have come to Britain from America in 1928 with others close on its heels. His grandfather, Walter, and father, Roy, trained lions to ride in the sidecars, as did the famous George "Tornado" Smith at Southend's Kursaal fairground. The Cripseys also developed a technique of being towed round behind the Indian Scouts on roller skates. "If you were competing side by side in a fairground, you always had to have one stunt better than the other," explains Graham. Smith also kept a skeleton in a sidecar which, with a flick on a control, would suddenly sit bolt upright. And Ricky Abrey, 61, who rode with him as "The Black Baron", says Tornado perfected a ride where three riders would cut off their engines at the top of the wall and instantly re-start them again, causing the audience to gasp as 2 ft–long flashes of flame escaped the exhaust pipes.

12 Fun, then, for all the family. "People still love the wall of death," says Ken Fox emphatically. "People like what we put on and get good value for it. If they see it once, they always want to see it again. The problem is finding the people to work on it. There are a lot of soft men around."

Write down four things the early wall of death riders included in their acts. [2|1|0]

Early wall of death riders included lions riding in their sidecars, a skeleton sitting upright in a sidecar, riders cutting their engines, and then restarting to them to produce alarming flashes of flame.

General question 3 (2006)

Read the following paragraphs:

15 In resignation, I ripped a piece of paper from my yellow notepad. My black ball-point pen shook slightly in my trembling right hand as I wrote out the fateful question: "Gloria, will you go out with me this Friday?" Beneath that monumental question, I drew two boxes. One was conspicuously large. I labelled it the YES box. The second box was tiny. I labelled it the NO box.

16 And that is the yellow piece of paper I have folded up into a square and am holding in my damp hand as I wait here on Torture Island for Mrs Moonface to turn towards the blackboard and give me the opportunity I need.

Quote two separate words used by the writer to suggest the importance of what the boy is asking Gloria. [2|1|0]

The words are 'fateful' and 'monumental'.

This time four things have been asked for – therefore to score 2 marks you must provide all four. Any three would be worth 1 mark, and, obviously, if you only provide 2 or 1 you get zero marks.

Let's go through the paragraphs looking for the things they included in their acts:

- *they trained lions to ride in their sidecars;*
- *some were towed round behind the Indian Scouts on roller skates;*
- *one person kept, in his sidecar, a skeleton which could sit bolt upright;*
- *three riders would cut their engines;*
- *they would instantly re-start them, causing 2ft-long flashes of flame to alarm the audience.*

All you have to do is choose any four of the above for full marks!

We need to look for words which have the connotations of importance or significance. In Paragraph 15 there is the word 'fateful', which suggests something important and significant, as does the word 'monumental', which suggests something colossal, of epic proportions.

Now try this

General question 4 (2006)

Read Paragraphs 15 and 16 in General question 3

Write down **three pieces of evidence** that suggest the narrator's nervousness at this point in the story. [2|1|0]

Questions about word choice and the connotations of words

Questions about word choice really involve your understanding of the **connotations** of words. Words have two levels of meaning: the denotative and the connotative. The **denotation** of a word is the object in the universe to which any given words refers. The word 'book', for example, can refer to this actual book. The **connotation** of a word, on the other hand, is what we associate with the word. For example, the word 'apple' has connotations of redness, juiciness, crispness, shininess, and so on, but it also connotes or suggests the fall of man, since, according to the Bible, Adam ate the apple of the forbidden tree of knowledge and as a consequence was expelled along with Eve from the Garden of Eden or Paradise.

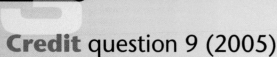

Credit question 9 (2005)

Look at Paragraph 2 in the extract below.

> 2 Kings, queens, princes, heads of state and generals have arrived and departed here. One of Naguib Mahfouz's earliest heroes, the ultra-nationalist anti-British rabble rouser, Saad Zaghul, escaped an assassination attempt at Cairo Station on his return from one of his numerous exiles, in 1924. Given Egypt's history of dramatic arrivals and departures the railway figures as a focal point and a scene of many riotous send-offs and welcomes.

How does the word choice of the opening sentence of Paragraph 2 help to convey the importance of Cairo Station? [2|1|0]

> The writer conveys the importance of Cairo Station by referring to high-ranking, important people.

*It is vitally important to recognise the task: **how does the word choice convey the importance of Cairo Station?** If your answer fails to show how the word choice conveys the importance then you will score no marks. Now the word 'how' means 'in what way(s)': you are being asked in what ways does the author by his word choice **in the opening sentence** convey the importance of the station. The opening sentence refers to many high-ranking people, with power or influence. In other words important people.*

Credit question 10 (2007)

Read the following extract from a Credit paper:

---

14 The young guide, Rob, was waiting outside. A workman's van hurtled past, then we crossed the road, entered through a wicket gate and followed a path across the field. We were walking toward the tomb by an indirect route that respected the wide ditch around the site. Sheep were grazing the field, and a heron was standing with its aristocratic back to us. There was a breeze, and the shivery call of a curlew descending. On all sides there are low hills, holding the plain between them. To the south, the skyline is dominated by two much bigger, more distant hills, a peak and a plateau. Though you wouldn't know it from here, they belong to another island, to Hoy. Above these dark hills, in horizontal bars, were the offending clouds.

Comment on the writer's use of word choice in her description of the clouds in the final sentence of Paragraph 14. [2|1|0]

The term 'horizontal bars' suggests that the light gets restricted.

or

The word 'offending' suggests that the clouds are in the wrong for restricting the light.

The task is to identify the word choice (1 mark) and then to examine the contribution of the word choice to the description of the clouds (1 mark).

The writer uses both 'horizontal bars' and 'offending' to describe the clouds, so what does each contribute? What does the term 'horizontal bars' make you think of, what are its connotations? You could say 'wall bars in a gymnasium' but that wouldn't be appropriate in a description of the clouds. What about prison bars – bars which entrap or restrict? The word 'dark' that the author uses about the hills suggests that light is being restricted or limited, presumably by the clouds.

We can analyse the connotations thus: the term 'horizontal bars', especially with its association with the ideas of horizon and distance, and the idea of a (prison) bar, all suggest the idea of the light being restricted. The author also calls the clouds offending, a clear use of personification, suggesting that the clouds were causing offence or were in the wrong for restricting the light.

1 mark for the reference and 1 mark for the comment in each case.

Credit question 11 (2001)

Read the following extract:

> 4 The driver opened the back door of the taxi and my "aunt", as we referred to her – really my mother's aunt's daughter – divested herself of the travelling rugs. She hazarded a foot out on to the gravel – in a pointy crocodile shoe – as if she were testing the atmosphere. She emerged dressed in a waisted black cashmere overcoat with a fur collar and strange escalloped black kid-skin gloves like hunting gauntlets.
>
> 5 I saw my mother noting again the black stiletto-heeled shoes with their red piping. The face we'd never seen was hidden under a broad-brimmed black felt hat, which I felt none of the women we knew in our closed circle would have had the courage to put on their heads.

(a) What impression of the aunt do you get from the writer's word choice of the words 'divested', 'hazarded', and 'emerged' to describe her movements? [2|1|0]

(b) What is added to this impression by his description of what she is wearing? [2|1|0]

> (a) These words suggest someone theatrical, who thinks she might be in some danger, and who is a show-off.
>
> (b) The description of what she was wearing suggests someone unusual and bold.

Now try this

The following extract has two questions. Read the questions carefully. The two questions are worded differently, but they are both about word choice.

Credit question 12 (2006)

Read the following paragraph:

> 19 Outside the Hyatt, a ragbag collection of protestors from the Simplified Spelling Society waving placards proclaiming "I'm thru with through" and "50,000,000 illiterates can't be wrong", pressed leaflets arguing for an overhaul of spelling upon dubious and somewhat non-plussed contestants.

What does the writer's use of the words 'ragbag collection' to describe the protesters suggest about his attitude towards them? [2|1|0]

'I'm thru with through' (Paragraph 19). Explain the **two** different spellings of the word 'through' on the protestors' placards. [2|1|0]

These words suggest someone theatrical (she doesn't just remove the travelling rugs, she almost strips them off her); someone calculating and affected (she doesn't just step out of the car, she pretends that there is possible danger, either to herself or to her shoes); she is attention-seeking and a show-off (she doesn't just get out of the car, she makes a gesture of it, aware that she has an 'audience').

The black cashmere overcoat with a fur collar and the strange scalloped black kid-skin gloves suggest wealth and self-confidence. The black stiletto-heeled shoes with their red piping and the broad-brimmed black felt hat suggest someone strange and exotic, someone unusual and full of poise and audacious (bold), especially since the writer comments that no women he knew would have the courage to put it on their heads!

Questions about the meaning of words

word n **1** smallest single meaningful unit of speech or writing. **2** chat or discussion. **3** brief remark. **4** message. **5** promise. **6** command – v **7** express in words.

Questions about the meaning of words are very easy to spot. You are usually asked to give the meaning of a word and say how the context helped you arrive at it. The context is invariably the sentence within which the word appears or the surrounding sentences – just use your common sense.

This kind of question crops up at Higher as well. What matters is being able to relate the context to the meaning.

Credit question 13 (2007)

Read the following paragraph:

> 1   The building nowadays known as Maes Howe is a Neolithic chambered cairn, a tomb where, 5000 years ago, they interred the bones of the dead. In its long, long existence it has been more forgotten about than known, but in our era it is open to the public, with tickets and guides and explanatory booklets. It stands, a mere grassy hump in a field, in the central plain of Mainland Orkney. There is a startling collection of other Neolithic sites nearby.

Give the meaning of 'interred' and show how the context helped you to arrive at that meaning. [2|1|0]

'Interred' means 'buried'. This is seen from the context, which says that Maes Howe was a tomb, where the bones of the dead were interred.

Look out for

If you are answering questions about the meanings of words, be sure to show how the context helped you arrive at the meaning if you are asked.

The text says the place was a tomb in which they interred the bones of the dead, then 'interred' must mean buried – you can then say that the words 'interred' and 'bones of the dead' suggest that 'interred' must mean 'buried' – that way you have shown how the context makes the meaning clear.

Look out for

Sometimes, you are simply asked for the meaning of a given word without having to refer to the context, though invariably the context will make the meaning clear.

Credit question 14 (2007)

Read the following paragraph:

2   To reach Maes Howe I took the road that passes over a thin isthmus between two lochs. On the west side is a huge brooding stone circle, the Ring of Brodgar. On the east, like three elegant women conversing at a cocktail party, are the Standing Stones of Stenness. The purpose of these may be mysterious, but a short seven miles away is the Neolithic village called Skara Brae. There is preserved a huddle of roofless huts, dug half underground into midden and sand dune. There, you can marvel at the domestic normality, that late Stone Age people had beds and cupboards and neighbours and beads. You can feel both their presence, their day-to-day lives, and their utter absence. It's a good place to go. It re-calibrates your sense of time.

'a thin isthmus' (Paragraph 2)

Tick the box beside the best definition of 'isthmus'.

area of land	
strip of land with water on each side	
stretch of moorland	
bridge connecting two islands	

[2|0]

area of land	
strip of land with water on each side	✓
stretch of moorland	
bridge connecting two islands	

The passage does say: I took the road that passes over a thin isthmus between two lochs *therefore the phrase* between two lochs *makes clear that an isthmus must be land that has water on each side.*

Now try this

Credit question 15 (2003)

Read carefully the following paragraph:

10   When the London dodo died, the animal was stuffed and sold to the Ashmolean Museum in Oxford. Taxidermy not being what it is today, over the next few decades the dodo slowly rotted until it was thrown out in 1755. All, that is, except the moth-eaten head and one leg.

Explain how the context helps you to understand the meaning of the word 'taxidermy' in Paragraph 10. [2|0]

Questions about sentence structure

Although questions about sentence structure are not asked every year, nevertheless they form part of what is known as questions about language – and such questions are very frequently asked at Higher. You therefore have to know and understand all about sentence structure.

We have already looked at sentence structure in Chapter 2, but here we will examine specific questions asked about sentence structure in Close Reading.

Sentence structure – when it is useful to know about adverbs

In Chapter 2 we looked carefully at adverbs and their function – let's now apply that knowledge.

Credit question 16

Read the following passage carefully:

> *A lot has been learned about the nature of cosmic collisions and this new knowledge has given a remarkable twist to the story of our origins. We now recognise that comet and asteroid impacts may be the most important driving forces behind evolutionary change on the planet. Originally, such objects smashed into one another to build the Earth 4.5 billion years ago. After that, further comet impacts brought the water of our oceans and the organic molecules needed for life. Ever since then, impacts have continued to punctuate the story of evolution. On many occasions, comets slammed into Earth with such violence that they nearly precipitated the extinction of all life. In the aftermath of each catastrophe, new species emerged to take the place of those that had been wiped out.*

How does the sentence structure in this paragraph draw attention to the writer's ideas?

Think carefully about how the writer uses adverbs of time at the beginning of several of his sentences. By placing these adverbs of time at the beginning of each sentence, the author draws attention to the stages by which this Earth and life on it were formed.

The first two sentences make clear that he is talking about the ways in which asteroid impacts over time had been the major force behind evolutionary change on this planet. Now examine carefully the remaining sentences. They all begin with an adverb or an adverbial phrase. They are all adverbs of time, marking a stage in a progressing timeline. The positioning of the adverbs draws attention to their meaning.

Take each adverb and adverbial phrase and examine the contribution to the argument:
- *Originally: adverb of time establishing the beginning of the process*
- *After: adverb of time denoting next stage in the process and modifying that*

The positioning of adverbs and adverbial phrases of time (or words to do with time) at the beginning of each sentence draws attention to the timeframe, the sequence and the consequence of the asteroid impacts.

Sentence structure – when it is useful to know about adjuncts and prepositions

Many adjuncts begin with a preposition: out, beyond, from, onto. Most of them form what we call prepositional phrases – such as beyond the sunset, in the morning, on the motorway, under the table, in the car. So now you know to look out for such phrases and if they are at the beginning of a sentence the chances are that attention is being drawn to them.

Now try this

Now try some for yourself. Comment on the effect on meaning of the structure of the following sentences – it will be easier if first of all you identify the adjunct(s):

> Out of the blue, she appeared early that morning.
> 'Beyond the next hill was Aswan.'
> 'Originally, such objects smashed into one another to build the earth 450 million years ago.'
>
> *'Bent double, like old beggars under sacks,*
>
> *Knock-kneed, coughing like hags, we cursed through sludge,*
>
> *Till on the haunting flares we turned our backs,*
>
> *And towards our distant rest began to trudge.'*

You can see that knowing about adverbs and prepositional phrases considerably enhances your ability to give a full answer.

- *Ever since then:* adverbial phrase of time, where *ever* is an intensifier (see page 17) drawing attention to the importance of what happened after that point in time
- *On many occasions:* prepositional phrase (see page 21) acting as an adverbial phrase of time and number, where *many* draws attention to the number of occasions when asteroid impacts have taken place
- *In the aftermath of each catastrophe:* another prepositional phrase acting as an adverb – in the aftermath of – drawing attention to the results of the impacts, followed by each catastrophe where *each* is an intensifier, stressing the significance of every single catastrophic asteroid occurrence.

Sentence structure – when it is useful to know about lists

In Chapter 2 we looked carefully at the different types of lists and their effects – let's now apply that knowledge.

Credit question 17 (2004)

Read the following paragraph:

> 2   The stranger wore the unidentifiable and ragged remains of a shirt and trousers, and a kind of surcoat cut out of animal skins that had been tacked together with thongs of sinew. Pelagia saw, beneath the table, that in place of shoes his feet were bound with bandages that were both caked with old, congealed blood, and the bright stains of fresh. He was breathing stertorously, and the smell was inconceivably foul: it was the reek of rotting flesh, of suppurating wounds, of dung and urine, of ancient perspiration, and of fear. She looked at the hands that were clasped together in the effort to prevent their quivering, and was overcome both with fright and pity. What was she to do?

'it was the reek of rotting flesh… fear'.

Explain fully how the writer emphasises the smell from the stranger by means of sentence structure. [2|1|0]

> The writer uses a list in parallel structure – by the repetition of the word 'of' before each item in the list, he creates a cumulative effect, drawing attention to the smell.

Credit question 18 (2007)

Read the following paragraph:

> 14   The young guide, Rob, was waiting outside. A workman's van hurtled past, then we crossed the road, entered through a wicket gate and followed a path across the field. We were walking toward the tomb by an indirect route that respected the wide ditch around the site. Sheep were grazing the field, and a heron was standing with its aristocratic back to us. There was a breeze, and the shivery call of a curlew descending. On all sides there are low hills, holding the plain between them. To the south, the skyline is dominated by two much bigger, more distant hills, a peak and a plateau. Though you wouldn't know it from here, they belong to another island, to Hoy. Above these dark hills, in horizontal bars, were the offending clouds.

Comment on the writer's use of **sentence structure** in her description of the clouds. [2|1|0]

> The positioning of the prepositional phrases at the beginning of the sentence (1 mark) creates a climactic build-up, drawing attention to the 'offending clouds' (1 mark).

Let's look at the sentence very closely: it was the reek of rotting flesh, of festering wounds, of ancient perspiration, and of fear.

You should be able to recognise that the structure is that of a list. But also notice the repetition of the of before each item, such that the structure of each item in the list is repeated – thus the list is said to be in **parallel structure***, the effect of which is cumulative. The list, therefore, is climactic in effect.*

Focus on the final sentence of the paragraph. Read it carefully. Remember what we said in Chapter 2 about the effect of changing normal word order? The sentence, were it in normal order, would read: The offending clouds were above the dark hills in horizontal bars. *The author has moved the two prepositional phrases –* above the dark hills *and* in horizontal bars *– to the beginning of the sentence thereby creating a climax. There is a build-up to the expression* were the offending clouds *thus drawing attention to the expression itself and reinforcing the fact that the clouds were in the wrong.*

Sentence structure – when it is useful to know about forms of sentences and about subordination

When you are answering questions about forms of sentences, it helps to remember that sentences can take one of **four forms**:

▶ Statement   I walk

▶ Interrogative   Do I walk?

▶ Imperative   Walk!

▶ Interjection   Gosh!

General question 5

Read the following paragraph:

From whence comes this compulsion to climb mountains? My neighbours seem to be able to enjoy lives of quiet contentment without ever having to leave the horizontal plane. Why do I have this compulsion to get to the top of every insignificant bump on the landscape? I ponder this question not in the hope of providing an explanation for my neighbours, still less in the hope of converting them, but out of a need to explain this outlandish behaviour to myself. If I am to climb mountains I would simply like to know why. Why, no matter how breathless, bruised, battered and bedraggled I become while hillwalking, do I return with a grin on my face and a desire to go out and do it again?

By referring to sentence structure, show how the author demonstrates his need to climb mountains. [2|1|0]

Now you try working out the answer.

Look carefully at the paragraph – note the author's use of questions. There are three of them, which suggest that he is doing all that he can to find an answer – by repeatedly questioning his need to climb mountains he is demonstrating and drawing attention to the very existence of his need.

Look at the final sentence. The straightforward comment about the structure of this sentence is that it contains a list: no matter how breathless, bruised, battered and bedraggled I become while hillwalking which is climactic and, by building up to the climax, draws attention to the discomfort and unpleasantness that he experiences but which does not stop him returning again and again to the hills.

This sentence is a good example of **subordination** (see page 22). The subordinate clause – no matter how breathless, bruised, battered and bedraggled I become while hillwalking – is embedded in the main clause – Why do I return with a grin on my face and a desire to go out and do it again? One of the effects of structuring the sentence in this way is not only to draw attention to the list (on which we have already commented) but also to create climax – the subordinate clause positioned where it is delays the main point – questioning his going out and climbing again and again – until the very end of the sentence.

Credit question 19 (1994)

Read the following paragraph carefully:

> 8   Little has really changed since the 18th century, I would imagine, at the auction by which, each morning at 8am, the trawlers dispose of their catch. The boats, rimmed still with frost and ice from the fishing grounds, mostly look antique themselves, and the fishermen look altogether timeless, stalwart, comely men, their faces rigid in the truest Scottish mould, unhurried, polite; and there the fish of the cold seas lie as they always did, cod, hake and flatfish, glistening in their wooden crates. Through all the hub-bub, the slithering of seaboots, the clattering of boxes, the chugging of engines, the shrieking of seabirds, the slurping of tea from enamel mugs, white-coated auctioneers immemorially grunt their prices, and lorries rumble away over the cobbled quays.

By close reference to the final sentence of the paragraph, show how the writer creates the impression of 'hub-bub' at the auction. [2|1|0]

Now you try working out the answer.

You can see that the final sentence is structured in the form of a list. (This type of list is called a **parenthetical list**.)

We have already looked at parenthesis when we examined punctuation. You need to know that parenthesis is the use of information additional to but not part of the syntax of an individual sentence. See page 30. In this case the sentence is Through all the hub-bub … rumble away over cobbled streets. The list – the slithering of seaboots, the clattering of boxes, the chugging of engines, the shrieking of seabirds, the slurping of tea from enamel mugs – is inserted between paired commas and is parenthetical. The point is that the items in the list reveal the extent and the variety of the activity and hence create the impression of hub-bub. But also look at the verbs – shivering, clattering, chugging, shrieking, slurping. What do you notice about them grammatically and what about the sounds they convey?

Look out for

Make sure you can identify a list and you can identify parenthesis!

Credit question 20 (1994)

Read the following paragraph carefully:

10 The crime rate is the lowest, as are the juvenile delinquency rate, and the vandalism rate, and the unemployment rate: and the educational standards are the highest, and the long beach promenade is entirely unvulgarized, and the town has won the Britain in Bloom contest so often that it has tactfully withdrawn from the contest. Aberdeen has an enterprising arts centre, municipally supported, and its high-rise buildings have been tastefully held in check, and its industrial development is discreetly zoned, and altogether it is in many ways the best of all possible burghs.

(a) What is unusual about the sentence structure of Paragraph 10

(b) What effect do you think the writer hopes to achieve by this structure? [2|1|0]

Now you try working out the answers.

! **Look out for**

When you are asked about sentence structure, look out for lists. About 90% of the time the answer is a list. But remember, there are various types of list.

Look at the first sentence. You can see right away that the sentence is in the structure of a list, but you also notice that there are conjunctions (in this case the conjunction is the word 'and') between each item in the list. We call such lists **polysyndetic lists**. (The device where an author uses many conjunctions is called polysyndeton.)

One of the effects of a polysyndetic list is to give equal stress to each item in the list. In this case, the polysyndetic structure stresses equally the low crime rate, the low delinquency rate, the low vandalism rate, the low unemployment rate, the high educational standards, the attractive state of the beach promenade, and the decision to withdraw from the Britain in Bloom contest. There is also a kind of cumulative effect created which draws attention to the absence of problems and the sheer delight of life in Aberdeen.

Credit question 21 (1996)

Read the following paragraph carefully:

> 5   Asya slopped through the slush, thinking of Spring. By the time she reached the middle of the river, the mist had enveloped her. The boathouse behind her was gone, and the long, smudged line of her water-filled steps trailed away into nothingness. The pencil line of the opposite shore had disappeared. She stood still and listened. A faint sound. A scythe being drawn against a sharpening-stone. A blade being honed on something hard. She turned around, sucking her mitten, trying to figure out which direction the sound was coming from. Blades scything, blades hissing, coming closer. Where had she heard that sound before? Then she knew. It was a skater, out there in the mist, coming towards her. No one she knew.

'She stood still and listened.'

(a) What two features of sentence structure does the writer use to convey the sound Asya hears? [2|1|0]

(b) What is the effect thus created? [2|1|0]

> Now you try working out the answers.

Now try this

General question 6 (2007)

Read the following paragraph carefully:

> 1   Henry had been impatient for the cast to be removed so that he could return to his job as the bender for Mr Hairston at the Corner Market. Mr Hairston had a back problem and found it hard to bend over. Henry did the bending for him. Picked up whatever fell on the floor. Reached for merchandise on the lower shelves to fill the customers' orders. He also had other duties. helping unload the boxes and crates that arrived from the wholesalers. Stocked the shelves. Bagged the potatoes in the cellar, then carried them upstairs to the produce section. Mr Hairston was proud of his produce. Fresh lettuce and carrots and spinach and such extras as parsnips and mushrooms, all of them in neat displays at the rear of the store.

How does the writer's use of sentence structure draw attention to the variety of actions that Henry has to carry out? [2|1|0]

To answer this one you have to reflect on everything we have learned about sentence structure in order to identify two features of structure. Two of the sentences A scythe being drawn against a sharpening stone and A blade being honed on something hard contain present participles; that is, the verbs in the sentences are non-finite, therefore the sentences are **minor sentences**.

There are three minor sentences, one after the other, all following on from She stood still and listened: *One of the features of sentence structure has to be the use of minor sentences, or sentences without main or finite verbs. The other feature is that the sentences are in the form of a list, listing what it is she heard as she listened. The effect is, as we have already suggested, that the sentences list what she heard. By not having main verbs, the effect is to focus on the sound and not any movement.*

There is another point you can make: the sentences are short and one feature of short sentences is their dramatic impact. Therefore the very shortness of the sentences draws attention to them and therefore to their meaning – in this case to the very sounds that Asya heard.

Now try this

Credit question 22

Read the following paragraph carefully:

Up in smoke

Can there be anything more truly, deeply wasteful than burning several thousand pounds in five minutes, and making a lot of noise as you do it? By virtue of their scarcity, fireworks used to be so magical: tracers of dreams in the sky. Now they're like bad television: ubiquitous, tacky, unoriginal, wearisome and dangerous in the hands of naughty teenagers. Numbed by excess, we no longer wonder at the colours of the sky set alight. We just close the curtains and comfort the old dogs who spend Friday and Saturday nights trembling in our arms.

From an article in The Herald by the columnist Melanie Reid.

(a) From your reading of the short article, what, in your opinion, is Melanie Reid's attitude towards Bonfire Night?

(b) In what ways does Melanie Reid's use of sentence structure help convey that attitude? [2|1|0]

Questions about sentence structure – when it is useful to recognise the length of the sentence

Look out for questions about sentence structure being asked in a different way.

General question 7 (2008)

Read the following paragraph carefully:

1   It was the stickers that gave it away. Turning left on the A9 at Latheron in Caithness, you were suddenly faced with a sign that looked as though it had been defaced by advertising executives from surfing companies. Like a cairn on a mountain path, the big green board declaring Thurso to be 23 miles away told travelling bands of surfers that they'd taken the right turn-off and were nearly at their destination. Slapping another sticker on the sign was like laying another stone on the pile.

2   Thurso is about to enter surfing's big league.

3   It's hard to reconcile the popular tropical imagery of surfing with the town, a raw, exposed kind of place that enjoys little escape from the worst excesses of the Scottish climate. The Caithness coastline is peppered with surfing spots, but the jewel in the crown and the target for dedicated wave riders lies within spitting distance of Thurso town centre at a reef break called Thurso East. In the right conditions, the swell there rears up over kelp-covered slabs into a fast-moving, barrelling monster of a wave considered world class by those in the know.

Now you can answer the question in different ways – as a question about word choice/connotations (of 'big league') or as a question about sentence structure.

'Thurso is about to enter surfing's big league.' (Paragraph 2) How does the writer make this statement stand out? [2|_|0]

He makes the statement stand out by making it a short one-sentence paragraph.

The term 'big league' suggests the ultimate in sporting competition, a dramatic climax of sporting competitive activity.

Sentence structure answer

Word choice/connotations answer

Look out for

Questions don't necessarily fit into neat compartments – so use your wits to make the 'best fit' you can!

Questions about link sentences

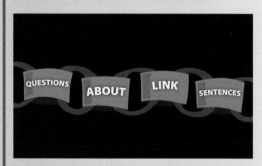

Questions about link sentences can be tackled using a simple method:

▶ in the link sentence in question, quote the words that link back and demonstrate what idea(s) they link back to, and then

▶ quote the words that introduce the new ideas and demonstrate which new ideas are introduced.

Credit question 23 (2006)

Read the following paragraph carefully:

> 10 Spellbound featured one boy, Neil, whose Indian immigrant father not only hired specialist tutors to coach his son in words derived from French and German but also paid for prayers to be said in India for him. Despite such dedication, Neil didn't win.
> 11 But the proclivities of those contestants and their parents in no way represent the general participant. "It's not just the geeks and the nerds. These are normal kids," says Ohio's Beth Richards, whose daughter, Bailey, was making her second appearance in the finals. "This is the Superbowl of words."

How does the first sentence of Paragraph 11 act as a link between Paragraphs 10 and 11? [2|1|0]

> The link is established by the word 'But', a conjunction which introduces a contrasting idea. The expression 'the proclivities of such contestants' links back to the actions of Neil's father while the expression 'in no way represent the general participant' anticipates the idea that participants are just 'normal kids'.

! Look out for

Be careful. Sometimes you are asked to show how a paragraph forms a link. You should answer it in the same way.

Firstly, the sentence begins with But *– a conjunction or joining word. The word* But *not only acts as a joining word but also introduces a statement which contrasts with the ideas in the previous paragraph. The word* But *begins the linking process.*

Secondly, the word proclivities *refers back to the idea of hiring specialist tutors, as mentioned in the previous paragraph.*

Thirdly, such contestants refers back to Neil, whose father hired specialist tutors to coach his son.

The link back to the previous paragraph has been established, but what about the link to Paragraph 11? The expression no way represent the general participant *introduces the notion that the general participants are* normal kids.

This answer is worth more marks than are available!

Credit question 24 (1995)

Read the following paragraphs carefully:

8 His father looked at the sweating horse, and after a pause he said that that would be all right. Howard could see he knew the berries weren't ready yet, like the ones behind the steading that they always picked; and he understood that this was a lesson being set up for him when he came home without brambles: not to tell lies. And there'd be another lesson behind this one, the real lesson: that his father had been right about that sort of new-fangled nonsense coming to grief.

9 In spite of this, he forgot it all and slipped through the Racecourse fence.

10 A crowd mobbed around the grandstand where they served drinks and sandwiches. He made his way through the high society of Lanark, dolled up to the nines and mingled with noisy, alarming foreigners. He wished he hadn't come. Then as no-one paid any attention to him, he wandered out among the planes. They were fragile and dazzling, the opposite of the solid farm carts. Sometimes the aviator would be sitting in the cockpit while a mechanic tried the plane's propeller. In others the mechanics tuned the engines. The air was full of roaring, the strange exciting smell of gasoline, and drawling voices talking of their kites.

Explain how the one sentence paragraph (Paragraph 9) is an effective link between Paragraphs 8 and 10. [2|1|0]

Now you try working out the answer.

The method is still the same:

- *identify the words that link back: in this case they are* In spite of this *(where the word* this *refers back to a word or idea – we say that such words take an antecedent – something which has gone before and to which the word refers);*
- *the words refer back to the ideas about which Howard has been thinking;*
- *the words* slipped through the Racecourse fence *introduce the idea of Howard attending the people and events at the racecourse.*

Now try this

General question 8 (2004)

Read the following paragraphs carefully:

Pucker way to kiss a hummingbird

Mark Carwardine puts on lipstick in Arizona for a wild encounter.

1 There's a rather embarrassing tradition in wildlife circles in certain parts of Arizona. Visiting naturalists are encouraged to try to "kiss" a wild hummingbird.

2 This is more of a challenge for men than it is for women – mainly because it involves wearing lots of red lipstick. A dress and high heels are optional, but the redder and thicker the lipstick the better. Hummingbirds drink nectar from flowers that are often bright red and have learned to associate this particular colour with food. They mistake your mouth for one of their favourite plants – at least, that's the theory.

Explain the way in which the first sentence of Paragraph 2 acts as a link between Paragraph 1 and Paragraph 2. [2|1|0]

Questions about figures of speech

The term **figures of speech**, also known as **literary devices**, refers to ideas such as metaphor, simile, personification, alliteration, and onomatopoeia. Read pages 25–27 in Chapter 2 to revise these figures of speech.

You need to know about figures of speech to help you answer questions in the Close Reading papers, but also so that you can use them as tools of analysis in your study of literature. You also need to make reference to them in your Critical Essays. The Grade Related Criteria for Credit levels Critical Essays require that the student 'demonstrates awareness of technique by analysis, using critical terminology' (i.e. literary devices) where appropriate.

Credit question 25 (2006)

Read the following paragraph:

> 6   But the competition really got going when the field was whittled down to the final two dozen spellers on day three. By then, contestants were beginning to struggle as they tiptoed, letter by letter, through their words as though they were crossing a minefield. "Vimineous" ended North Carolina's Simon Winchester challenge.

'as though they were crossing a minefield'

(a) Identify the figure of speech the writer is using here. 2|_|0

(b) **In your own words**, explain how appropriate you find the use of this image. [2|1|0]

The expression is 'as though they were crossing a minefield' – in other words the figure of speech is a simile because it uses 'as'. Similes are much more explicit than metaphors: a simile makes the comparison very clear by its use of 'like' or 'as'.

contestants were beginning to struggle as though they were crossing a minefield

Term A   *Term B*

how do you cross a minefield?
carefully, gingerly, tentatively,
one foot wrong and instant death,
unsuspected danger all around.

The contestants were struggling in the same way as if they were crossing a minefield – carefully aware of the fact that one mistake and they are instantly out of the contest.

Credit question 26 (2005)

Read the following paragraph:

> 5   To leave the enormous sprawling dust-blown city of gridlock and gritty buildings in the sleeper to Aswan was bliss. It was quarter to eight on a chilly night. I sat down in my inexpensive First Class compartment, listened to the departure whistles, and soon we were rolling through Cairo. Within minutes we were at Gizeh – the ruins overwhelmed by the traffic and the bright lights, the tenements and bazaar; and in less than half an hour we were in the open country, little settlements of square mud-block houses, fluorescent lights reflected in the canal beside the track, the blackness of the countryside at night, a mosque with a lighted minaret, now and then a solitary car or truck, and on one remote road about twenty men in white robes going home after prayers. In Cairo they would have been unremarkable, just part of the mob; here they looked magical, their robes seeming much whiter on the nighttime road, their procession much spookier for its orderliness, like a troop of sorcerers.

'like a troop of sorcerers' (paragraph 5 – end).

Explain the effectiveness of this simile. [2|1|0]

> In this simile, the word 'troop' suggests an organised group or a group with a purpose and the word 'sorcerers' suggests that the group has magical powers or looks weird.

The author has been talking about the 'twenty men in white robes going home after prayers' and he compares them with 'a troop of sorcerers'.

Let's be clear about the literal meanings of the word 'troop':
- a military unit, comprising soldiers
- a unit of boy scouts
- the collective noun for certain animals – monkeys, for example.

The idea of a group of people organised for a specific purpose is suggested.

The literal meaning of 'sorcerers', as people with magical powers, suggests something supernatural, weird, mystical.

Now try this

Credit question 27 (2007)

Read the following paragraph:

> 2   To reach Maes Howe I took the road that passes over a thin isthmus between two lochs. On the west side is a huge brooding stone circle, the Ring of Brodgar. On the east, like three elegant women conversing at a cocktail party, are the Standing Stones of Stenness. The purpose of these may be mysterious, but a short seven miles away is the Neolithic village called Skara Brae. There is preserved a huddle of roofless huts, dug half underground into midden and sand dune. There, you can marvel at the domestic normality, that late Stone Age people had beds and cupboards and neighbours and beads. You can feel both their presence, their day-to-day lives, and their utter absence. It's a good place to go. It re-calibrates your sense of time.

Identify the figure of speech used by the writer to describe the Standing Stones of Stenness. What does it suggest about the stones? [2|1|0]

Questions about writer technique

Questions about writer technique can take a variety of forms but they usually do contain the word 'writer' which helps identify them. The answers demand knowledge about language and figures of speech. (See Chapter 2 to revise figures of speech.)

General question 9 (2006)

Read the following paragraphs:

22 Suddenly Mrs Moonface stops lecturing.

23 Her right hand, holding the chalk, rises.

24 Then her hips begin to pivot.

25 This all unfolds in very slow motion. The sheer importance of the moment slows the action, way down.

26 The pivoting of Mrs Moonface's hips causes a corresponding rotation in the plane of her shoulders and upper torso.

27 Her neck follows her shoulders, as day follows night.

28 Eventually, the lunar surface of her face is pulled towards the blackboard.

29 She begins to write. I have no idea what she is writing. It could be hieroglyphics and I would not notice. It could be a map of Blackbeard's treasure and I would not care.

30 I am now primed. My heart is thumping against my ribs, one by one, like a hammer pounding out a musical scale on a metal keyboard. Bing. Bang. Bong. Bam. I am breathing so quickly that I cannot breathe, if that makes any sense.

31 I am aware of every single one of my classmates in Maths.

32 Everyone in Maths is now preoccupied. There are only four minutes left in the period. Mrs Moonface is filling up blackboard space at an unprecedented speed, no doubt trying to scrape every last kernel of mathematical knowledge from the corncob of her brain before the bell. My classmates are racing to keep up with her. All around me pens are moving across notebooks at such a rate that ink can barely leak out and affix itself to paper.

33 My moment is at hand! The great clapper in the bell of fate clangs for me! Ka-wang! Ka-wang!

The obvious answer is sentence structure (the use of very short sentences and short one-sentence paragraphs), but it is not the only answer. You could also identify the techniques of simile and metaphor. Work out the simile in Paragraph 30, the metaphor in Paragraph 28 and the extended metaphors in Paragraph 32.

There are also examples of other literary and linguistic devices, such as onomatopoeia, alliteration, and hyperbole. Let's look at onomatopoeia first: the words Bing. Bang. Bong. Bam. attempt to imitate the actual sound of a hammer pounding on the keyboard. But we have also to say how the words Bing. Bang. Bong. Bam. suggest John's growing excitement. The vowel sounds Bing. Bang. Bong. Bam. suggest an increasing noise, culminating in the final Bam. The increasing noise suggests his increasingly loud heartbeat and therefore his increasing excitement. The same sequence features alliteration: the repetition of the B sound words Bing. Bang. Bong. Bam. Here it is used to express increasing noise and therefore increasing excitement.

Continues on page 63.

(a) Identify **one** technique used by the writer in this section to suggest John's growing excitement. [2|1|0]

(b) Explain **how** it does so. [2|1|0]

Now you try working out the answers.

Now try this

General question 10 (2006)

Read the following paragraphs:

> 5 But luckily, she does not call on me. She has a piece of chalk in her right hand. She is waving it around like a dagger as she spews algebra gibberish at a hundred miles a minute.

How does the writer make Mrs Moonface's behaviour seem threatening? [2|1|0]

General question 9 – contd.

The other example of onomatopoeia, Ka-wang! Ka-wang! is used to capture the noise of the bell. The narrator says that it's the bell of fate that clangs (more onomatopoeia) for him, which is very exciting since his fate is about to be revealed. Not only is clang an example of onomatopoeia, but the whole sentence – The great clapper in the bell of fate clangs for me – is an example of hyperbole. Identify the other examples of hyperbole in Paragraph 32. The clear suggestion of exaggerated speed contributes to the suggestion of his growing excitement.

Note the use of minor sentences: Bing. Bang. Bong. Bam. What is the effect created? Remember that you have to relate your answer to the idea of John's growing excitement.

Questions about punctuation

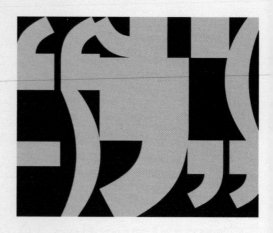

Questions about punctuation are not frequent, but they do appear from time to time. It is important for you to recognise the function of most punctuation marks, and to be able to use them accurately and precisely to make your meaning clear.

General question 11 (2007)

Read the following paragraphs:

> 3   But within 30 seconds he was back on his feet – calmly spelling a-l-o-p-e-c-o-i-d to much applause. Buddiga recovered sufficiently to go on to the final rounds of the competition.

Why does the writer separate the letters in this word with dashes? [2|1|0]

Now you try working out the answer.

In this particular case, you have to use your common sense – the fact that the competitor is 'calmly spelling a-l-o-p-e-c-o-i-d' makes clear that the dashes indicate the way in which the competitor spelled the word, a letter at a time, or the way in which he pronounced the letters aloud.

General question 12 (2007)

Read the following paragraphs:

> 13   "Wall of death" is, thankfully, a bit of a misnomer, for there have been no fatal accidents on British walls, though whether that's due to good luck or fear-induced careful preparation is difficult to tell. "I've been knocked off by other riders, the engine's stalled, I've had punctures and I've hit a safety cable," says Ken Fox, pointing at his scars. "Everyone gets falls at some time but we try to be spot-on in our preparations. Before every show we spend a complete day trying to get the machines working perfectly."
>
> 14   Luke Fox suffered his first bad fall last year, flicking a safety-cable bolt on one of his "dips" as he zig-zagged his bike up and down. He fell 20 ft, got up and started again, even though he'd severely torn his knee. In a sense, he's got his own good-luck charm. His Indian bike was originally ridden by no less a daredevil than Tornado Smith himself. Luke has also inherited his father's total dedication to the trade and the Fox family wall looks set to last into the immediate future. Indeed, he and Kerri are now a partnership, sharing the long-haul driving and other things, while young Alex, the ferret-fancier, is raring for his first go at the wall.

Why is the word 'dips' in inverted commas? [2|_|0]

'Dips' is in inverted commas to show that it is a technical word.

In this case, the inverted commas signal that the word is a technical word – a word used by the riders, particularly the term used by Luke Fox.

Questions about tone

Examiners know that candidates find questions about tone difficult, therefore such questions aren't often asked at Standard Grade (though they are frequently asked at Higher). When they are asked the answer is often 'humour' since that is an easy tone to identify.

Ironic, sarcastic, and sardonic humour

Answering questions about tone is easier if you know about irony, sarcasm, and sardonic humour. These kinds of humour are easier to spot than they are to define but the following explanations may help.

Irony, at its simplest level, is when someone says something that he doesn't mean, thus revealing some absurdity. What is said often involves exaggeration, and it often involves absurdity or even some kind of inconsistency.

Irony has to do with the user's awareness of the gap between words and their meanings and/ or between an action and what is implied by that action – for example, there is something highly ironic about a boy being severely punished for not being able to recite a section of the Bible on the powerful ability of love to forgive all things. In this latter case, the irony is probably further heightened by the fact that the punisher is most probably unaware of the ironical nature of the situation.

In **irony of situation**, language isn't necessarily involved: for example, where someone has, with her first cup of coffee in the morning, a cigarette and a vitamin pill.

Sarcasm is much easier to spot and to define, since sarcasm involves ridicule. It still entails someone saying something that he doesn't mean, but this time in order to ridicule another person or a situation. For example, in response to the teacher's question the boy gives an entirely wrong answer to which the teacher responds: 'Oh, well done, Darren, what a clever boy!' – and the rest of the class laughs. The teacher certainly did not mean that Darren was clever, just the opposite.

Sardonic humour is perhaps more subtle than sarcasm, but it still contains the notion of mockery.

Credit question 28 (2006)

Read the following paragraph:

> 13 He appeared close to hyperventilating as he started slowly then rattled through the word, confident that, after three days of ruthless competition, the grand prize was his. Blinking in amazement, he appeared overwhelmed, burying his face in his hands as his mother rushed the stage to embrace him. "It's kind of sad I won't be able to be in more spelling bees," says Tidmarsh. The tears welled in his eyes as he contemplated the awful void that lay ahead. Unlike boxers or basketball stars there's no second coming or return from retirement available to champion spellers. Former winners are not eligible to enter.

'…the awful void that lies ahead of Tidmarsh.' (Paragraph 13)

(a) What is the 'awful void' that lies ahead of Tidmarsh? [2|_|0]

(b) What tone is the writer adopting in the expression? [2|_|0]

> (a) The awful void is because there are no more spelling competitions.
>
> (b) The tone is ironic or humorous.

The answer to (a) is quite easy, and getting it right enables you to answer the second and more difficult part of the question – identifying the tone of the remark made by the writer.

The awful void is the fact that he cannot enter any more spelling bees now that he has won the National competition – there is nothing ahead for him, nothing to fill the time that preparation and the events themselves have taken up, nothing but emptiness ahead.

The term awful void does seem a bit of an exaggeration and since it is being used by the writer about Tidmarsh, we can be fairly sure that he is being ironic: the author doesn't actually mean that there is a void, awful or otherwise, in front of Tidmarsh. He is being humorous.

General question 13 (2006)

Read the following paragraphs:

6 I hear nothing. Algebra does not have the power to penetrate my feverish isolation.

7 You see, I am preparing to ask Glory Hallelujah out on a date.

8 I am on an island, even though I am sitting at my desk surrounded by my classmates.

9 I am on Torture Island.

10 There are no trees on Torture Island – no huts, no hills, no beaches. There is only doubt.

11 Gloria will laugh at me. That thought is my lonely and tormenting company here on Torture Island. The exact timing and nature of her laughter are open to endless speculation.

12 She may not take me seriously. Her response may be "Oh, John, do you exist? Are you here on earth with me? I wasn't aware we were even sharing the same universe."

13 Or she may be even more sarcastic. "John, I would love to go on a date with you, but I'm afraid I have to change my cat's litter box that night."

14 So, as you can see, Torture Island is not exactly a beach resort. I am not having much fun here. I am ready to seize my moment and leave Torture Island forever.

Look at Paragraphs 11 to 14.

(a) Write down an example of the writer's use of humour in these paragraphs. [2|_|0]

(b) Explain why your chosen example is funny. [2|1|0]

Now you try working out the answers.

The important thing here is to choose examples that you can effectively explain. There is no point in selecting some item of humour if you then can't say why it is funny.

You have been provided with Paragraphs 6 to 10 by way of context and also because there are other language points to discuss. These are her responses:
(i) 'Oh, John, do you exist?';
(ii) 'Are you here on earth with me?';
(iii) 'I wasn't aware we were sharing the same universe.';
(iv) 'John, I would love to go on a date with you, but I'm afraid I have to change my cat's litter box that night'.

It's probably easiest to explain why (iv) is funny. The idea that the girl of his dreams would prefer to do something as unpleasant as empty a cat's litter tray rather than go out with the narrator is really quite amusing.

The humorous aspects of (i) to (iii) lie in the fact that her questions and comments are a bit ludicrous given that he is in the same class.

Questions about conclusions

It is impossible to set out examples of questions about conclusions since you would need to have the whole passage in front of you and space won't allow that. But here are some guidelines which should make these questions easier to tackle. When you come across a question about conclusions, look for:

▶ a word or word group that signals summing up

▶ a single sentence or paragraph that has dramatic impact

▶ a build-up to a climactic ending

▶ a humorous or surprising point that is also summative

▶ any link back to the very opening of the passage

▶ any example or anecdote that illustrates the points the author has been making.

If you keep these points in mind, then the question should be very easy to answer. It's a question about technique – you don't have to repeat the ending, you have to demonstrate how the final paragraph concludes the passage.

Now try this

Credit question 29 (2008)

Read the following paragraphs carefully:

5   She was one of those children possessed by a desire to have the world just so. Whereas her big sister's room was a stew of unclosed books, unfolded clothes, unmade bed, unemptied ashtrays, Briony's was a shrine to her controlling demon: the model farm spread across a deep window ledge consisted of the usual animals, but all facing one way—towards their owner—as if about to break into song, and even the farmyard hens were neatly corralled. In fact, Briony's was the only tidy upstairs room in the house. Her straight-backed dolls in their many-roomed mansion appeared to be under strict instructions not to touch the walls; the various thumbsized figures to be found standing about her dressing table—cowboys, deep-sea divers, humanoid mice—suggested by their even ranks and spacing a citizen army awaiting orders.

6   A taste for the miniature was one aspect of an orderly spirit. Another was a passion for secrets: in a prized varnished cabinet, a secret drawer was opened by pushing against the grain of a cleverly turned dovetail joint, and here she kept a diary locked by a clasp, and a notebook written in a code of her own invention. In a toy safe opened by six secret numbers she stored letters and postcards. An old tin petty cash box was hidden under a removable floorboard beneath her bed. In the box were treasures that dated back four years, to her ninth birthday when she began collecting: a mutant double acorn, fool's gold, a rain-making spell bought at a funfair, a squirrel's skull as light as a leaf.

Now answer the following questions:

In Paragraph 5, the writer develops a contrast between Briony and her big sister.

(a) In your own words, state what the contrast is. [2|1|0]

(b) By referring to sentence structure, explain how this contrast is developed. You must refer to both characters (and be sure in all such questions about contrasts to refer to both sides of the contrast in your answer). [2|1|0]

(c) By referring to punctuation, explain how this contrast is developed. You must refer to both characters. [2|1|0]

(d) By referring to word choice, show how this contrast is developed. You must refer to both characters. [2|1|0]

Twice in Paragraph 5 the author uses the paired dash.

(e) Explain the function on both occasions.

(f) What is the effect of using this punctuation device on both occasions? [2|1|0]

(g) 'Another was a passion for secrets': (Paragraph 6) Show how the writer continues this idea in the rest of the paragraph. [2|1|0]

(h) Explain the function of the colon in the expression 'when she began collecting:' [2|1|0]

(i) Comment on the structure of the second sentence of Paragraph 5? [2|1|0]

Since this is really a word choice question, you really must make close reference to the words that develop the idea of passion for secrets.

You may have to look back to Chapter 2 to remind yourself about clauses.

Now you try working out the answers.

Developing a broad range of writing skills

Your Standard Grade course and assessments will enable you to develop a number and a variety of writing skills. Your Writing Skills are tested in your Folio work and in the exam.

For your Folio, you have to produce;

- three critical essays in response to the literature you have studied

- two essays, one of which has to be of a transactional (discursive or argumentative) nature, while the other must be a personal or creative essay.

In the exam, the Writing Paper which will test your ability to compose an essay from one of a variety of topics.

You will already have had a great deal of practice in writing essays. We will examine in detail the demands of the actual assessments in later chapters, but in this chapter we'll have a look, generally and specifically, at all that is involved in becoming a good writer. Developing these skills will improve your chances of achieving a Credit Grade.

Reasons for writing!

There are, of course, many reasons for writing. We write in order to take notes; we write in order to set out instructions; we write, maybe in the form of a letter, in order to express our point of view about something; we often, especially once in employment, have to write reports; and sometimes we write to create a piece of imaginative work, a dramatic sketch, a novel, a short story, or a poem for example.

You'll be relieved to know that reading and writing are very closely related skills. The more that you practise the one, the more you will improve the other. For example, as you learn the reading skill of analysing the effect of placing prepositional phrases at the beginning of sentences, so you can start to adopt that technique in your own writing. It's the same with the use of lists, subordination, metaphor – in fact, with all the reading skills that we examined in Chapter 3. You should now try incorporating some of these skills into your written work.

Let's examine writing skills under four headings: the reader, register, structure, and style.

Look out for

The Credit GRC state that you are expected to use an 'accurate and varied' vocabulary – so make sure that you do!

The reader

It is really important that, whatever it is you are writing, you always know *why* you are writing and *who* you are writing for. For example, imagine you're on holiday and you decide to send one of your friends a postcard. As you sit down at the cafe to compose your message, two aspects of writing skills are already fulfilled:

▶ you already know your reader (your friend) and

▶ you know the purpose of your writing (to tell your friend how much fun you are having).

As you write the purpose may change: you may decide that you will make your friend jealous by exaggerating how much you are enjoying yourself!

Look out for

So here's a first guideline: writing to someone specific helps focus your writing.

Register

Register is the term we use to describe a group of words and phrases appropriate to a given topic, subject matter or theme. For example, we associate the words 'pupil', 'assembly hall', 'teachers', 'Morning, sir', 'Please, miss', 'dining hall', 'classroom', 'examinations' with school. Other words for register are **diction** and **semantic field**.

Register also applies to the language we consider appropriate for a given audience. We often switch register almost automatically, since we are aware that our audience determines a certain appropriateness of language. For example, when you relate an incident that happened in school, you will fairly automatically switch registers when you tell the story to your best friend, then to your parents, and finally to the rector. You recognise that the kind of language (vocabulary, sentence structure, and style) that is appropriate for your friend's ears just might not be quite so appropriate for the rector's.

It's the same with texts and emails, where the mode – the nature of texts and emails (speed, space constraints, informality) not only creates its own register but also creates the opportunity for a different kind of spelling where vowels can replace entire words ('u' for 'you'), numbers can replace words ('2' for 'to') and replace syllables (as in 'str8' for 'straight', 'm8' for 'mate', and 'b4' for 'before'). Sometimes vowels are completely omitted ('txt' for 'text' and 'rtn' for return) and sometimes letters are used to stand for entire words ('brb' for 'be right back' and 'lol' for 'lots of laughs' or 'lots of love').

English is an ever-changing language, developing all the time, but you also have to guard against the inappropriateness of certain language uses. For example, the register that may well be appropriate for texts and emails is probably totally inappropriate for a formal essay!

In every case, the audience – the person to whom you are writing your piece (teacher, examiner, friend, your local MSP, newspaper, job application) – will determine the register and formality of your language. It's interesting that some DJs have a particular person in mind when they broadcast; you could well adopt the same strategy when you write. Write your essay *for* someone and bear that person in mind as you continue writing. That will always keep the **purpose** of your writing in sharp focus.

Structure

Once you know who your reader is and why you are writing, you then need to decide on the structure of your piece. Whether it is a piece of personal writing, a short story, a poem, a newspaper article, a short dramatic sketch, a recipe, a set of instructions for the doggy-sitter, you have to set it out so that your reader can follow clearly what you have written. The structure has to support, and can even enhance, the subject matter.

With transactional writing – instructions, setting out an argument or discussion, conveying information – the structure needs to be logical. One idea or set of instructions has to follow another in logical sequence, and to do that successfully you have to think of the ways in which you can link paragraphs. Such writing tends to be formal.

When it comes to imaginative writing or even personal writing, you need to think about the ways in which you can use time as the basis of your structure. We live in time – that seems obvious enough – therefore when you are presenting a story of whatever kind you must think *time*. Stories have a beginning, a middle, and an ending. But unlike real life, where events tend to follow one another in a random, haphazard, almost accidental way, fiction has to be constructed in a deliberate way, where the author chooses events in order to create effect and support the idea or theme that he or she wants to present.

And of course because you are in control and choose everything that happens, you, as the author, don't have to adhere to the beginning–middle–end structure: you can rearrange it and use flashback where the structure is middle–beginning–end, though you can't ever alter where the ending comes!

A very important aspect of structure of fiction (our concern here is the short story) is the narrative technique or structure that you decide to use. In fiction, there are several 'points of view' – ways in which an author decides to tell a story. Here are the most important ones:

▶ **omniscient narrative point of view** where you create an all-knowing narrator who understands, directs, and relates all that is happening to all of the characters at all times

▶ **first person point of view** where the story is told by one of the characters, maybe even by yourself

▶ **third person point of view** where you focus your story on one of the characters such that all the events are seen through that character's point of view.

There are other points of view, which we will examine in detail when we come to the literature section in Chapter 7. For your own writing purposes, these three should suffice.

Structure also applies to the structure of paragraphs and individual sentences. In Chapter 2 you learned much about sentence structure (see pages 16–19). You learned about the importance of word order in a sentence and the effect of altering normal word order, especially by placing adverbs or adverbial phrases at the beginning of sentences for effect. You also learned about the effect of using adverbs (use them instead of peppering your writing with adjectives) and about the use of subordination, where you place the subordinate clause at the beginning of the sentence for effect, which also tends to be the marker of more formal writing. On the other hand, the use of minor sentences tends to be the measure of informal prose.

Then there are the various kinds of lists, all part of sentence structure: polysyndetic, asyndetic, lists in parallel structure, lists in climactic order. You should practise using them – the effect can be dramatic.

Style

The difference between structure and style has exercised scholars for many decades. Let's think physically to begin with. Look carefully at your room at home. Working out its **structure** isn't that difficult: you would measure its length, its breadth, its height, note where the window is situated, its dimensions, and any other physical aspects of the room's design. Its **style**, on the other hand, is the way in which you have decorated it: colour scheme, the positioning of the furniture, what posters you have and how they are set out, what curtains or blinds you have chosen for the window.

Stories are not that dissimilar: the structure of a story (or poem or play) is the way in which it has been put together, how each part of it relates to the whole. Structure, especially of fiction and dramatic texts, is one of time sequence, whereas the structure of non-fiction tends to be its internal logic. Poetry is more complex, but you have to be aware of verse structure, rhythm and rhyme (or lack of it).

Style is the way in which you 'decorate' your story. In Chapter 2 you learned about grammar and the use of language, and in Chapter 3 we examined carefully the various techniques used by writers to create effect. We looked at such techniques from the reader's perspective – to help you in your Close Reading and in your analysis of written texts in general. But remember what we said about the cyclical nature of reading and writing? As you improve your reading skills, so you improve your writing skills and so on? Now it's time for you to apply those reading skills to your own writing.

You need to be aware of **figures of speech**: not only should you consider the powerful effects that metaphor and simile can create, but you should also turn your attention to alliteration, hyperbole, and onomatopoeia.

You should also be aware of the function of various **punctuation** marks and symbols. The use of the colon or the semi-colon can add considerably to the style of your writing, especially if you are writing a formal, discursive piece. Too many candidates employ the *comma splice*, where they use a comma (wrongly) to join two units of related sense into one sentence. The misuse of the comma makes the writing appear illiterate, whereas had the writer used (correctly) a semi-colon, the writing would have appeared sophisticated and stylish. The use of the colon to introduce a list or an explanation makes your writing look both professional and controlled.

> The colon and the semi-colon are underused and much underrated punctuation marks – so, use them!

And then there is the question of tone. Your tone, like the register you choose, has to be appropriate to the reader and for the subject matter. Use humour, if it's appropriate; or irony or sarcasm. It could be that your tone has to be hectoring or persuasive or declamatory or formal or weary or irate. Don't overdo tone, but be aware of its effect.

Perhaps, most importantly, you must employ as wide a vocabulary range as possible – and that means you have to start building up your vocabulary. The English language contains over a million words; your active vocabulary range – the vocabulary items you actually use – is probably just a fraction of that, therefore you need consciously to increase and enrich your active vocabulary. We all recognise the meaning of more words than we use: or to put it another way, our passive vocabularies are greater than our active ones. But you need to develop your active vocabulary. Buy an A5 or an A6 notebook in order to record all those vocabulary items with which you are unfamiliar. Look such words up in the dictionary and write down their meanings in this notebook – and learn to use the words. Even use the notebook to remind yourself of words that you could use in your own writing.

Then you need to make sure that you conclude your piece effectively. You should signal your conclusion by words such as 'Finally…' or 'Therefore it can be seen that…' or 'Afterwards…' or whatever is appropriate for the kind of writing you have produced. Maybe, for a discursive piece, you conclude with an illustrative anecdote that sums up concisely and briefly everything you have been saying.

And finally, when it comes to composing a really powerful conclusion, it can be very striking to begin the final sentence with an 'And' (despite what we'd been told at Primary school), since that can clearly signal, especially where the author has used delaying mechanisms (inserted phrases and even parentheses), a build-up to a final, memorable, dramatic climax.

Practice makes perfect!

The Writing examination is one hour and fifteen minutes long and is sat by all candidates at whatever level: Foundation, General, and Credit. In the last chapter, we dealt with writing skills in a general way. In this chapter, we shall look at ways of making sure you get the best possible mark in your Writing paper. Always bear in mind that writing improves enormously with practice – so make sure you put in the time and effort to practise all the writing skills. Such endeavour will pay dividends in your Writing paper.

In the examination, you are presented with a booklet containing about 20 writing options, from which you have to choose one. On the left-hand side of each page of the booklet you will find a photograph and on the opposite page there will be a number of topics all related in some way to the photograph and to the overall topic suggested by the photograph. The final page of the booklet presents a number of topics with no photographs.

Demands of the Writing Paper – what markers are looking for

Let's first look at what the examiners are looking for in your Writing paper essays. The very first instruction to markers (in their marking instructions) is that to attain a Credit the candidate's writing will be distinguished by a detailed attention to the purposes of the writing task. In other words, before all else, the marker will be looking for **relevance** to the **purpose** of the task set, and there are four such purposes.

Look out for

It is vitally important to be completely relevant throughout your essay!

No matter how well you write, if you produce a personal essay when the task asks for discursive writing, you will be penalised, and you could end up with a grade 5 or worse, with the comment 'few signs of appropriateness'. The best advice is to urge you to be careful and pay attention to relevance.

The Writing purposes

The four **purposes** of writing are:

▶ to convey information

▶ to deploy ideas, expound, argue and evaluate

▶ to describe personal experience, express feelings and reactions

▶ to employ specific literary forms (e.g. short story, letter, poem).

Although there are usually more than 20 options, they all can be reduced to the four purposes of writing as set out above, and you must pay close attention to the demands of each. Remember that relevance is everything.

!Look out for

If you choose an essay that asks you to deploy ideas, you have to pay close attention to the **purpose** of such an essay. Not only that, but you must also pay attention to the **wording** (rubric) **of the task set**.

Conveying information

If you choose an essay which invites you to **convey information** then you must have some knowledge of the topic in order to give substance to your essay. Your essay must be informative, while at the same time presenting your views on the subject. Any personal anecdote that you introduce must support your line of thought. Remember, this isn't a personal essay.

Deploying ideas, expounding, arguing and evaluating

If you choose an essay topic which invites you to **deploy ideas, expound, argue and evaluate**, then you must present a clear, straightforward point of view. Your essay must be well structured, presenting an argument that:

▶ agrees with the topic

▶ argues against it, or

▶ presents a balanced view.

What matters is that you write formally and with a clear line of thought, supported by evidence. You need to know about the topic, be logical without necessarily being objective (you can take sides). Probably, it would be best if you had some opinions concerning the topic beforehand.

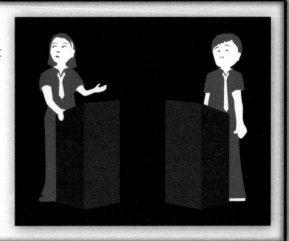

Personal experience essays

A **personal experience** essay, unlike the other three writing purposes, does not have to satisfy the demands of a particular essay type. You must, however, make sure that your essay is specific to and appropriate for the demands of the task.

Employing specific literary forms

You have the option to choose one of a number of specific literary forms, including the short story and the poem.

If you choose to write a **short story**, then you must pay attention to the short story genre – that is, you must demonstrate an understanding of narrative technique, and, as appropriate, you must show an aptitude for handling plot, setting, and character. Your short story must reflect the title that you are given or that you have chosen. A pre-prepared short story, made to fit a title, is unlikely to do well.

If you choose to write a **poem**, you must pay attention to the purpose indicated in the task, and (as appropriate) demonstrate your ability to express your feelings, explore the topic imaginatively, and be skilful in your employment of poetic and linguistic devices. You must also show clearly that you understand the structure of a poem and be at ease with poetic conventions. Good advice might be to steer clear of writing a poem in the exam unless you already know that you are a skilled poet!

Grade Related Criteria and the writing purposes

The Grade Related Criteria set out the things the markers are looking for when they mark your work. When approaching each essay, markers are told to bear in mind the ways in which the candidate displays the following aspects of essay writing (depending on the task attempted):

▶ knowledge

▶ insight

▶ imagination

▶ sustained development

▶ accurate and varied vocabulary

▶ accurate and varied paragraphing

▶ accurate and varied sentence construction.

The table below shows the difference in the standards expected from Credit level work and General level work.

	Credit	General
As the task requires, the candidate can	convey information, selecting and highlighting what is most significant	convey information in some kind of sequence
	marshall ideas and evidence in support of an argument; these ideas have depth and some complexity; he/she is capable of objectivity, generalisation and evaluation	order and present ideas and opinions with an attempt at reasoning
	give a succinct account of a personal experience: the writing has insight and self-awareness	give a reasonably clear account of a personal experience with some sense of involvement
	express personal feelings and reactions sensitively	express personal feelings and reactions with some attempt to go beyond bald statement
	display some skills in using the conventions of a chosen literary form, and in manipulating language to achieve particular effects.	use some of the more obvious conventions of a chosen literary form, and occasionally use language to achieve particular effects.

For a Grade 1 Credit award

To gain a Grade 1 for a Credit essay:

▶ An informative essay must convey information in a clear sequence, where the most significant aspects of the topic are carefully selected and highlighted.

▶ A discursive essay must be well structured, showing a depth of understanding, an ability to handle complex ideas and skill at setting them out.

▶ A personal essay must be well structured, revealing perceptiveness, self-awareness, and an ability to reflect on the experience. The very best personal essays reveal a real sense of the writer's personality.

▶ A short story has to be skilfully structured, revealing real distinction, proficiency, and adeptness in handling the short story form. Your use of language must be appropriate and pleasing, and stylish (sophisticated and impressively accomplished).

For a Grade 3 General award

The hallmark of a Grade 3 essay is that it is reasonably attempted rather than successfully achieved; such essays, though mainly technically correct, will tend to be dull and lack variety in language skills.

Precision and accuracy

The Grade Related Criteria also set out the requirements for precision and accuracy.

	Credit	General
Intelligibility and correctness	Writing which the candidate submits as finished work communicates meaning clearly at a first reading. Sentence construction is accurate and formal errors will not be significant.	Writing which the candidate submits as finished work communicates meaning at first reading. There are some lapses in punctuation, spelling and sentence construction.

Note the term 'finished work': the GRC are exactly the same for your Folio writing pieces as for the Writing examination. 'Finished work' clearly applies to the Folio pieces where you have months of preparation allowing you to draft and re-draft in order to perfect the 'finished work'. In the exam, you only have an hour and a quarter in which to read the entire booklet, make your choice, plan your essay and then write it. But you should still leave time at the end to go over your work, making corrections and altering phrases and sentences to make them accurate or more focused.

Look out for

English is a very complicated language and all of us make linguistic errors: you need to check your work carefully.

How to attempt the discursive or informative essay

A discursive or informative essay question in the Writing paper will give you a piece of stimulus material, and you have to write your response. For example, the stimulus material might be something like this:

Act Your Age!
There are fewer chances today simply to be yourself.

Give your views

This looks a bit like an invitation to write a personal essay, but beware – it does state clearly and in bold: **Give your views**. Hence this is a discursive or informative topic, and if you write a personal essay you could drop a grade, no matter how well written it is.

Read the information carefully!

Although the title *Act Your Age* provides a clue as to the content of your essay and, to a certain extent, the tone, the real substance of your essay is suggested by the next line: *There are fewer chances today simply to be yourself.* And therein lies the danger – it seems to suggest an invitation to write a personal essay all about self-analysis.

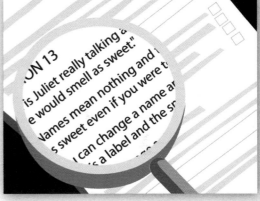

But it isn't – this is a discursive essay asking you to agree, disagree, or provide a balanced argument about the complexity of being oneself or being young in modern society. Think about the different ways you could approach this topic:

▶ The phrase 'fewer chances to be yourself today' suggests that in previous times it was possible to be yourself but that today it is much more difficult: one route into the essay might be to argue that in today's society we need to play a variety of different roles in order to be accepted.

▶ Or maybe you want to explore the line that in modern society there are so many demands and pressures on us, especially on the young, that we are unable to be truly ourselves, able to do whatever we want.

▶ Or it could be an interesting line of thought to examine how and why it is very difficult nowadays to be young (to act your age) simply because there are so many demands on and temptations for the young to act older than they actually are.

▶ Or your line of thought might be that it's difficult nowadays for the middle-aged and elderly to act their age since they feel the need to present a more youthful image.

However you care to explore the idea that there are fewer chances for people to act their age in modern society, there is nothing at all to stop you from drawing on your personal experience – what else have any of us got to draw on when we write? You can even relate anecdotal material, but it can only be used to support your argument or line of thought. What is most crucial is that you have to have a distinct and developed line of thought running through your essay, and that you can marshal (assemble) evidence (including, perhaps, an anecdote or two) in support of that line of thought.

Grade Related Criteria

The Grade Related Criteria set out the requirements for a Credit level answer:

The work displays some distinction in ideas, construction and language. This is shown by a detailed attention to the purposes of the writing task; by qualities such as knowledge, insight, imagination; and by development that is sustained. Vocabulary, paragraphing and sentence construction are accurate and varied.

What about a plan?

Of course everyone tells you that you need a plan, but don't dismiss the advice. A plan really is an essential part of your writing. It doesn't have to be extensive or complex, just a way of enabling you to create and sustain a structure for your essay. It will help you maintain focus and keep you on the right lines, preventing you from wandering into irrelevance.

For example, in your essay your plan might follow this structure:

Introduction	Make clear the chosen topic and establish your line of thought, setting out your stance – say, that the demands and pressures on young people are so great that they cannot truly be themselves
Main body (several paragraphs)	Develop the argument for not being able to be yourself – you establish the pressures – evidence from school, academic success, peer pressure, technology, fashion, need to be socially successful, thoughts about the future: self, family, friends, the planet… lack of time – always have to be thinking of what lies ahead
	Reflect on the fact that previous generations may have had more chance to be themselves – no tv, no computers, no mobile phones, less competition – but is that true: two world wars, poverty, emerging consumer society, the first teenagers, the increasing need to conform?
Reflection	You argue that part of the problem is lack of time: you quote W H Davies' famous lines – 'What is this life if, full of care, We have no time to stand and stare.'
	Quick thoughts on these lines – the solution to being yourself?
Conclusion	Briefly draw the lines of your argument together and sum up – illustrative anecdote?

Technically, you have to display not only accuracy in your sentence construction but also variety: you have to show that, however long your sentence, you have complete control over its syntax. Remember what we said about subordination? Its use, especially in discursive essays, gives your writing a sophisticated and formal appearance.

 **Look out for**

Pay attention to your conclusion! Make it concise and memorable: after all, it's at the end of your essay that the mark goes!

One more thing: take great care with the introduction. In other subjects, it may be necessary to state in your introduction what you are going to write about, but in English, it is better, especially in discursive and informative essays, to keep yourself out of it. There is nothing actually wrong with beginning: 'I am going to write about the difficulties of being yourself in modern society' but your essay will have a more adult, stylish feel to it if you avoid the use of the first person pronoun. You can begin: 'Increasingly, young people in the 21st Century are finding it difficult to be themselves.'

How to attempt the short story and the poem

If you choose either of these writing types, you must know about the form of each of them. In the case of the short story, the tasks will most frequently impose a title, which has to be reflected in your narrative. It could also be that the task imposes an opening, which must be continued.

Grade Related Criteria

The table below shows the different criteria required for Credit level work and General level work. You can see the importance of being able to use, as appropriate, the short story, letter or poetic form. You also have to be adept at using form, structure, and language to create meaning and effect. Quite a tall order.

	Credit	General
The candidate can:	display some skills in using the conventions of a chosen literary form, and in manipulating language to achieve particular effects.	use some of the more obvious conventions of a chosen literary form, and occasionally use language to achieve particular effects.

We'll look at an actual essay title and examine how to tackle it. You select the following topic:

> **Write a short story** using the following opening:
>
> *The reluctance was written all over John's face. He tugged at his mother's hand. He winced. He grimaced. He complained. Still his mother led him on …*
>
> *You should develop **setting** and **character** as well as **plot**.*

Where to begin!

The trouble is that it is very difficult to think up a plot: even Shakespeare, who wrote 37 plays, never produced an original plot, but 'borrowed' them from the Ancients. If it was impossible for the greatest ever dramatist to put together a plot, how much more impossible is it for you to concoct one in an hour and a quarter! You therefore really have to rely on a formula that you have thought out beforehand.

Plot has to involve events in a time sequence, but the events, as well as being linked in time, must also be linked causally.

Where to begin! – continued

Look out for

When you write your short story, then, you have to avoid merely telling a story, setting out events in time sequence. You have to build in ways in which the events are linked by cause. But you also notice that the queen died 'of grief': in other words, emotions are involved as well.

The oft-quoted example is:

The king died and then the queen died.

This is a story in the same way that a news item is a story. One event follows the other in time.

On the other hand, this is a plot:

The king died and then the queen died of grief.

The death of the queen is a consequence of the death of the king.

We are told why she dies – as a consequence of a prior event – and that's what makes it a plot.

Characters

Just as plots are difficult to think up in a short time, so are characters. How do you create characters who are believable in a short space of time under examination conditions? The answer is that you don't! You can base them on people you know, including yourself! That's not quite as surprising (or as ruthless) as it seems.

It's actually very difficult even for the best novelists to create characters out of nothing. Most novelists base characters, however loosely, on people they know – and you should do the same. In the short story you have chosen, the mother could be based on your mother, or on someone else's mother if yours is too gentle. 'He tugged at his mother's hand' suggests that John is quite young – it's unlikely that you, a young adult, would be tugging at your mother's hand… So who is John? You when you were younger? Your little brother? Someone else's little brother? He is obviously being dragged somewhere to which he doesn't want to go. First day at school? Visit to the dentist? Going to meet an overbearing aunt?

Or could it be (shades of 'Billy Elliot') that she is dragging John off, aged 8, to ballet lessons? He thinks it's going to be cissy – until he spots the girl of his dreams, who is also doing ballet. But he is poor at ballet and gets kicked out of the class and hangs out with his friends on the streets. Eventually, however, he impresses her by his break-dancing skills, is then spotted by a tv producer and goes on to fame and fortune.

Maybe John's mother drags him to an audition for the X-Factor or for a tv commercial – she is a horrendously pushy mum who has show-business ambitions for her young reluctant son.

Whatever situation or setting you decide, John is obviously being taken somewhere against his will ('reluctance was written all over John's face') and words such as winced and grimaced and complained all suggest John's age – and a certain tone. Be imaginative, but keep your setting and characters firmly grounded in your own experience.

You are maybe already getting the idea that although short stories aren't easy to compose quickly, nevertheless they can be fun – especially if you know that you are skilled in the art of the short story.

How to attempt an actual essay – personal writing

The personal essay is the most popular of writing choices.

Grade Related Criteria

The table below shows the different criteria required for Credit level work and General level work.

	Credit	General
The candidate can:	express personal feelings and reactions sensitively.	express personal feelings and reactions with some attempt to go beyond bald statement.

Again, we'll take an actual example:

Write about an occasion when your loyalty to a friend was pushed to the limit.

Remember to include your **thoughts and feelings**.

The freedom of the personal essay!

Since the personal essay does not belong to any particular essay type, it means there aren't any specific requirements to be met. It is almost impossible to be irrelevant when writing personally, though you must pay attention to the individual question. In the above case, for example, you must deal with the idea of your loyalty to a friend being pushed to the limit. And you note that it does say **an occasion** which means you are restricted to one particular occasion, though, of course, there can be a build-up to that one occasion or there could be some scenes all of which, nevertheless, are related and contribute to that particular occasion.

But what is comforting about the choice of a personal essay is that whereas the other essay types demand some knowledge of the topic or of the short story form, the personal essay demands only knowledge of yourself – and you have that in abundance.

Know yourself

You also must pay attention to the instruction to include your thoughts and feelings. In other words, you have to deal with your reaction to and reflection on the experience demanded by the rubric. A rambling account of something vaguely to do with the way in which a friend's behaviour tests your loyalty is insufficient. Your essay must be structured – in time – and must have some kind of climactic build-up. Obviously it has to be based on personal experience but it doesn't have to be wildly dramatic. It does have to express some kind of reflection on the event – what you learned, how you felt, in what way the experience did – or did not – change your attitude. In this case, did the friend remain a friend? Did it affect what you understand by the nature of friendship? Did it cause you to reflect further on yourself and your attitude to your friends?

Above all, do try to avoid shallow thoughts and emotions as well as the cloyingly sentimental. Be yourself!

To gain a Credit Grade 1, you must show some measure of insight and understanding of the experience. And there needs to be some kind of self-awareness even if implicitly expressed. Pay attention to vocabulary and sentence structure: your vocabulary should be extensive and apt, words well chosen for their precision and articulacy; your sentence structure should show variety and a certain liveliness. The best personal essays reveal the personality of the writer, maybe a slightly self-effacing quality or a self-deprecatory stance imbued with a touch of humour (check out the vocabulary!).

Now try this

You are now set the task of writing your own personal essay on the above topic. Before you begin you ought to set out a plan:

Introduction	You reflect on the nature of loyalty: serves a useful cultural purpose in that groups loyal to each other had greater chance of survival; same with family loyalty.
Introduction	in a more modern context, you reflect on the expectations that friendship involves loyalty.
Main body	Introduce your friend, and the nature of the friendship prior to the act of disloyalty.
	Describe the act of disloyalty itself – your friend does something of which you disapprove but you feel to say something would be an act of betrayal; you are forced to choose between your friend and family, or school authorities, or police; you are forced into making a choice, the outcome of which is that you could be in trouble; your friend reveals some secret to a third party, thus testing your loyalty to her or him. Whatever example you use, you must capture the idea that it is **your** loyalty to her or him that is tested and that it is tested **to the limit**.
Reflection	The outcome or resolution
Conclusion	Try to avoid the tagged-on speech about what you learned from the experience – it's your **thoughts** and **feelings** that should run through the essay.

The above is only a suggestion which you can and should alter to suit your own experience and predilections (preferences).

The main point is that you should always plan your writing – however briefly. The benefit of a plan is that it keeps you relevant and avoids your omitting important points.

The requirements of the Folio

This chapter will deal with writing essays for the Folio. Essays written for your Folio must fall within the same four writing purposes as the exam essays discussed in Chapter 5:

- to convey information
- to deploy ideas, expound, argue and evaluate,
- to describe personal experience, express feelings and emotions,
- to employ specific literary forms (e.g. short story, letter, poem).

The Folio writing tasks you submit have to be clearly identified: the two essays you finally submit for your Folio have to be clearly labelled **W1** and **W2** with titles and tasks spelled out.

A **W1** task involves either an **informative piece** of writing or a **discursive piece**.

A **W2** task involves either an **imaginative piece** or **personal writing**.

There is an important difference between the Writing paper you sit in May and the Folio: time! In the Writing paper, you have one hour and a quarter to compose an essay. For the Folio, you have months to complete two essays and you get to choose your own topic and rubric.

W1 Informative writing

You need to choose what kinds of essay to write for your W1 task. If you choose an informative piece, you might choose to set out a recipe, for example, but that's not very challenging and might not attract a Credit grade. You could choose to do a piece of biography that could turn out to be very interesting. It would involve some research if the person you are going to write about is famous, but there is no reason why you can't do a biography of your grandmother!

Should you choose biography you have to make it interesting, and that isn't so much down to your chosen character as the quality of your writing itself. A poor biographer can make the most colourful and interesting character utterly dull simply by weak vocabulary and monotonous sentence structure.

An example of a good biography

The following is the opening of James Shapiro's biography of a year in the life of William Shakespeare. We have to accept that Shapiro did his homework and knows all the details of the winter of 1598, but poetic licence allows some imaginative input to make the text lively and grab the reader's attention.

Although we are examining the following in order to improve your writing skills, nevertheless we have to use our reading skills to analyse how the writer achieves his effects.

The weather in London in December 1598 had been frigid – so cold that ten days before New Year the Thames was nearly frozen over at London Bridge. It thawed just before Christmas, and hardy playgoers flocked to the outdoor Rose theatre in Southwark in record numbers. But the weather was turning freezing cold again on St John's day, the 27th, and a great snowstorm blanketed London on 28 December.

As the snow fell, a dozen or so armed men gathered in Shoreditch, in London's northern suburbs. Instead of the clubs usually wielded in London's street brawls or apprentice riots, they carried deadly weapons – 'swords, daggers, bills, axes and such like'. Other than the Tower of London, which housed England's arsenal, about the only places to come by some of the larger weapons were the public theatres, where they were used to give a touch of realism to stage combat.

Look out for

Remember that we established that improving your reading skills can improve your writing skills and hence further improve your reading skills? Here is that process working in practice.

Look at Shapiro's use of detail: all December the weather had been frigid, it had been so cold that the Thames was nearly frozen over and we are given details of location: near London Bridge. The author makes the reader intensely aware of the cold, the returning cold, and the great snowstorm. This is a perfect example of the author using a natural condition – the weather – to establish atmosphere and also to reflect the human condition, because as the snow fell the preparations for street battle began. Look also at the detail in the second paragraph – all atmosphere and excitement.

Another part of the success of this piece is its ability to surprise – you most certainly don't expect men to fetch arms from a theatre! The reader's interest is instantly engaged.

The reader is drawn into the story – as you must draw your reader into your story of whatever character you choose to write about by the use of detail and atmosphere.

Note also the linkage between the two paragraphs: 'As the snow fell' links back to the great snowstorm and 'a dozen or so armed men' introduces the gang of fighters.

Look out for

Good linkage is a vital part of your essay since it gives the essay cohesion.

Shapiro uses lively detail: they carry deadly weapons. But he doesn't leave it at that – he develops the idea by listing the kinds of weapons: swords, daggers, bills, axes, and such like.

An example of a travel piece

Your informative essay could also be a travel piece about a place you have visited – not as a personal essay but as one which informs the reader of somewhere exotic. Obviously, it would be better if you had visited the place and have some first-hand information about it. The following is by the travel writer, Jan Morris, and describes her visit to Andalucia in the south of Spain:

We are in the Spanish South. The castanets click from coast to coast, the cicadas hum through the night, the air is heavy with jasmine and orange blossom, the soil is rich red or raw desert, there are prickly pears at the roadside, the girls have black eyes and undulating carriages, and often there hangs upon the evening the sad but florid strain of cante jondo *– the 'deep song', part Oriental, part Moorish, part Jewish, that the gypsies have made the theme music of the south.*

Note the comparison between the very short introductory sentence and the long sentence that follows. But look at the control the writer has over the syntax of the second sentence: it is very long, runs to the end of the paragraph, and is mostly structured as a list. In fact, it is a compound-complex sentence: a list of main clauses from 'The castanets click' to 'undulating carriages', followed by another main clause 'and often there hangs upon the evening' to the end of the list 'part Jewish', which in turn is followed by a subordinate clause, all so cleverly and rhythmically controlled.

The first list is in asyndetic structure, creating a climax, building up to the girls have black eyes and undulating carriages. But also look at the sheer variety of items in the list, from castanets (sound) to cicadas (sound) to jasmine (smell) and orange blossom (smell and colour) to the soil being rich red (colour) and the raw desert (visual and tactile) to prickly pear (visual, suggestion of tactile). What a variety of sounds and colour and smells, all suggesting the exotic nature of Spain. As do the connotations of the words – castanets, cicadas, jasmine, all suggest Spain and heat. She ends the list with the girls, which, with their black eyes and undulating carriages (the swing of their hips), create a highly sensual, appealing image.

Look out for

You would do well to imitate any of the various styles identified above!

The second list is interestingly constructed because it uses post-modification: the main word group is 'deep song' and the adjectives (the modifiers) come in a list *after* that word group (hence *post*-modification), thus creating a variety of structure as well as vocabulary.

W1 Discursive writing

The other kind of W1 writing is the discursive essay. Perhaps the greatest difficulty pupils face concerning the discursive essay is finding a subject to write about. Here are a few guidelines: above all, you should choose a topic in which you are interested and about which you have opinions. Some people will advise you to avoid what they call hackneyed or clichéd subjects, topics such as vivisection, genetic engineering, school uniform, capital punishment, euthanasia, but if you are really interested in and have knowledge of any of these subjects then you should express your opinions about any one of them.

Look out for

What makes an essay interesting is not so much the subject as the liveliness of the writing. Any discursive essay has to be well structured, logically progressed, and arrestingly introduced.

Life provides the material!

We live in interesting times. Concerns about how best to protect a liberal democracy against terrorist threats, street violence, gang culture, legal and illegal drugs abuse have never been higher. There are very real worries about the environment, the dependency on fossil fuels, the causes and effects of climate change, how to feed an increasingly starving world, racism, increasing technological advances, and, perhaps just as troublingly, the rapidly changing nature of society.

How to get going – generalised statements

You can begin your essay in a variety of ways. There is the opening that begins with a generalised statement and goes on to develop a more particular exploration of the subject.

As an example, here is an opening from a chapter of Stephen Fry's book *The Ode Less Travelled*. In it, Fry introduces the importance of understanding metre in poetry.

When we want to describe anything technical in English we tend to use Greek. Logic, grammar, physics, mechanics, gynaecology, dynamics, economics, philosophy, therapy, astronomy, politics – Greek gave us all those words. The reservation of Greek for the technical allows us to use those other parts of English, the Latin and especially the Anglo-Saxon, to describe more personal and immediate aspects of life and the world around us. Thus to be anaesthetised by trauma *has a more technical, medical connotation than to be* numb with shock, *although the two phrases mean much the same. In the same way,* metre *can be reserved precisely to refer to the poetic technique of organising rhythm, while words like 'beat' and 'flow' and 'pulse' can be freed up for less technical, more subjective and personal uses.*

He begins by making a generalised statement about the influence of Greek on our language, especially our technical vocabulary, persuading the reader that the study and understanding of poetry requires a technical vocabulary just as other disciplines require and use technical vocabulary. Again, note the use of the list right at the beginning. Interestingly, his paragraph is as informative as it is discursive, while setting out the outline of his line of thought.

How to get going – particular statements

Sometimes discursive writing begins with the particular and goes on to examine the subject in more general terms. Newspaper opinion writers, often referred to as columnists, invariably begin articles in this way in order to gain the reader's interest.

The following is the introduction to an essay by the journalist Ian Bell in *The Herald*. The opening paragraph is of a very general nature, covering the Beijing Olympics, the economy at home, and war and the threat of war overseas. The second paragraph narrows the possible topics to the media and the Olympics.

> *Beijing bonhomie has kept a great many newsreaders going through the dull, dreich days of a British August. At home, the horizon has been suffused in economic gloom. Abroad, war and the threat of war have dominated a meagre news agenda.*
>
> *But never fear: here's word of another Olympic gold to lift the mood and fill the airtime for which the BBC, in particular, has paid a good deal of money.*

Note the use of alliteration in 'Beijing bonhomie' which draws the reader's attention right at the very beginning, but also note the structure of the next two sentences: they are in parallel structure, both beginning with adverbs of place, thus drawing attention to the near and the far, thus contributing to the generalised nature of the statements. He goes on to develop what he sees as the relationship between the Olympics and the media.

Presenting an argument

Let's look at a slightly different kind of discursive essay – one which isn't so much exploring an issue as presenting an argument. The following is the introduction to an article by Ruth Wishart, a columnist with *The Herald*:

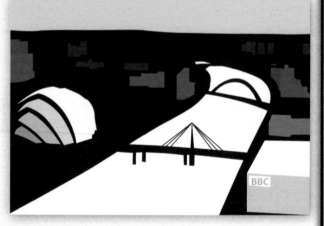

> *If you hail from Glasgow you will have friends or relatives whose roots lie in the Irish Republic. You will have Jewish friends or colleagues — whose grandparents, a good number of them Polish or Russian, may have fled persecution in Europe. You will eat in premises run by Italian or French proprietors. It is a diverse cultural heritage enriched now by a large and vibrant Asian population and a smaller but significant Chinese one.*
>
> *It was not always thus.*
>
> *The city census of 1831 found 47 Jewish citizens, a community which grew and prospered as it became an integral part of Glasgow's merchant growth. The first Asian immigrants were no more than a few young men, largely from poor and rural backgrounds, whose early employment as door-to-door salesmen gave no hint of the entrepreneurial flair their heirs and successors would bring to so many trade sectors in the city.*
>
> *The early Italians found the route to Glaswegian hearts through their stomachs as they set up chains of chip shops, and ice-cream parlours. The Chinese too helped the local palate become rather more discerning when they began to arrive in numbers half a century ago.*
>
> *All of these immigrant populations have two things in common: they were economic migrants and their effect on their adopted homeland has been, almost without exception, a beneficial one.*

Presenting an argument – continued

In the first paragraph, Wishart uses the second person pronoun (the 'you') in order to involve the reader and, perhaps, persuade 'you' to her point of view: that we are all acquainted with people who come from countries other than our own, and that the immigrants from these countries are vibrant and have brought a diverse cultural heritage which has enriched our way of life. Look at the connotations of the word choice, all positively supporting her point of view.

You have to admire her use of the single sentence paragraph, which so carefully links the ideas in the first paragraph to the idea that immigrants weren't always here in such profuse numbers, as developed in the second paragraph. The single sentence paragraph is not only structurally important as a link, but it is also quite dramatic.

The second paragraph shows the extent of Wishart's research and grasp of the facts – always important in discursive writing. The paragraph is also an important plank in her argument – that immigrants, even when few in number, have always been an essential part of Glasgow's economic expansion. The third paragraph reinforces that stage of the argument by suggesting that their contribution was not only economic – it was also culinary and educative. The fourth paragraph confirms that immigrants have always been economic migrants and that their contribution to Scottish society has been very largely to our advantage. You can see the build-up of the argument and you can probably work out where it is going to go: countering prevailing attitudes to immigrants in general and asylum seekers in particular.

Look out for

Reading the columnists of quality newspapers will undoubtedly enhance your ability to compose discursive essays!

The table shows some useful words and phrases when presenting an argument

Word / Phrase	Meaning
But	Introduces contrasting idea
However	Introduces a possible exception to the point being made
Furthermore	Elaborates on the point being made
Moreover	Intensifies the point being made
Although x is the case, y is also the case	Despite the point just made, we should also consider the following
Additionally	Another point…
Not only…but also	Intensifies the idea that there is further evidence that…
On the other hand	Here is another point of view, another way of thinking about the issue
On the one hand…on the other hand	Balancing two points of view

W2 Imaginative and personal writing

You have also to consider the W2 writing demands of the Folio: the imaginative piece or the personal piece. The imaginative piece can take the form of a short story or a poem. Unless you've been told that your poems are particularly good, however, you should probably avoid the poem and stick to a short story. Personal writing often gives you more freedom about what you want to write, but there are still rules and guidelines you need to be aware of.

Imaginative writing – the short story

We will start with the short story form. The marking instructions make clear that 'the development of **character** and **setting** as well as **plot** is an **explicit requirement** for all the short story option'.

Establishing character

In the following extract, we can see how Somerset Maugham establishes the character of the verger in his short story of the same name.

The Verger

There had been a christening that afternoon at St. Peter's, Neville Square, and Albert Edward Foreman still wore his verger's gown. He kept his new one, its folds as full and stiff though it were made not of alpaca but of perennial bronze, for funerals and weddings (St. Peter's, Neville Square, was a church much favoured by the fashionable for these ceremonies) and now he wore only his second-best. He wore it with complacence for it was the dignified symbol of his office, and without it (when he took it off to go home) he had the disconcerting sensation of being somewhat insufficiently clad. He took pains with it; he pressed it and ironed it himself. During the sixteen years he had been verger of this church he had had a succession of such gowns, but he had never been able to throw them away when they were worn out and the complete series, neatly wrapped up in brown paper, lay in the bottom drawers of the wardrobe in his bedroom.

Place and the character's name are instantly established: Albert Edward Foreman. What does that name suggest? Maugham lived from 1874–1965, so it's possible the name 'Albert' suggested Prince Albert, the consort to Queen Victoria, just as the verger is a 'consort' to the vicar. 'Edward' is another royal name – suggestions of tradition, stoicism, dignity, formality. Then we have 'Foreman', the name for a person in charge of a gang of labourers, with working class connotations. We therefore immediately get the impression that this man, possibly of working class origins, has a traditional outlook on life and a formal manner.

The word complacence in this context means that he wore the gown with satisfaction; it doesn't have its more modern suggestion of smugness.

Look how Maugham creates the character

Look out for

When you create a character, think carefully of the name you give him or her, since the name, as with many of Dickens' characters, can suggest the kind of people they are.

so economically – 'the dignified symbol of his office' suggests that he takes great pride in his job as verger, he sees it as an office; 'he took pains with (his) gown' suggests that he takes great care of things; 'he pressed it and ironed it himself' – he is fastidious and assiduous; he couldn't throw old gowns away but kept them 'in the bottom drawers of his wardrobe' at home confirming that he is traditional and embraces change reluctantly, holding on to the past. And it's all done with just a few phrases.

Establishing character, setting and atmosphere

Let's now see how another short story writer, Will F Jenkins, establishes setting, character, and atmosphere in 'Uneasy Homecoming'.

Connie began to have the feeling of dread and uneasiness in the taxi but told herself it was not reasonable. She dismissed it decisively when she reached the part of town in which all her friends lived. She could stop and spend the evening with someone until Tom got home, but she didn't. She thrust away the feeling as the taxi rolled out across the neck of land beyond most of the houses. The red, dying sun cast long shadows across the road.

So far, their house was the only one that had been built on the other side of the bay. But she could see plenty of other houses as the taxi drew up before the door. Those other houses were across the bay, to be sure, but there was no reason to be upset. She was firm with herself.

The taxi stopped and the last thin sliver of crimson sun went down below the world's edge. Dusk was already here. But everything looked perfectly normal. The house looked neat and hospitable, and it was good to be back. She paid the taxi driver and he obligingly put her suitcases inside the door. The uneasy feeling intensified as he left. But she tried not to heed it.

Try working out how Jenkins establishes setting. Look carefully at the first paragraph, where he effectively establishes time and place. When is it set? What is the effect of the images 'red', 'dying sun', 'shadows'? Exactly where is it set?

Read again the second paragraph. How does Jenkins *develop* time and place? In what ways does the setting establish loneliness? Then examine how he establishes and develops the character of Connie.

First person narration

Your short story can be in the first person, where you create a character to narrate your story. As we said before, humour can enhance your story considerably. Look at this highly satirical piece by Dorothy Parker, a New York writer in the 1920s and 1930s: the extract is from a short story, written in the form of a week's diary entries. The entry for Wednesday is produced here.

continued

Imaginative writing – the short story – continued

During days of Horror, Despair and World Change

Wednesday. The most terrible thing happened *just this minute.* Broke one of my finger nails *right off short.* Absolutely *the* most horrible thing I ever had happen to me in my life. Called up Miss Rose to come over and shape it for me, but she was out for the day. I do have the worst luck in the *entire* world. Now I'll have to go round like this all day and all night, but what can you do? *Damn* Miss Rose. Last night too hectic. "Never Say Good Morning" too foul, *never* saw more poisonous clothes on the stage. Took Ollie up to the Ballards' party; *couldn't* have been better. They had those Hungarians in the green coats and Stewie Hunter was leading them with a freesia – *too* perfect. he had on Peggy Cooper's ermine coat and Phyllis Minton's silver turban; *simply* unbelievable. Asked *simply sheaves of divine* people to come here Friday night; got the address of those Hungarians in the green coats from Betty Ballard. She says just engage them until four, and then whoever gives them another three hundred dollars, they'll stay until five. *Couldn't* be cheaper. Started home with Ollie, but had to drop him at his house; he *couldn't* have been sicker. Called up the new number today to get him to come to dinner and go to the opening of "Everybody's Up" with me tonight, but he was tied up. Joe's going to be out, but didn't condescend to say *where of course.* Started to read the papers, but nothing in them except that Mona Wheatley is in Reno charging *intolerable cruelty.* Called up Jim Wheatley to see if he had anything to do tonight, but he was tied up. Finally got Ollie Martin. Can't decide whether to wear the white satin or the black chiffon or the yellow pebble crepe. Simply *wrecked* to the core about my finger nail. Can't bear it. Never knew *anybody* to have such *unbelievable* things happen to them.

Look how she uses Italics, not just for emphasis but to capture the way in which the character actually speaks the Italicised words and phrases. How else does she capture the spoken language? What do you notice about the sentence structure of 'Broke one of my finger nails *right off short*'? What is missing? Is that structure repeated and, if so, what is the effect? What do you notice about the kinds of things that upset her? What kind of impression of her do you begin to form?

What comment can you make about the title? In what way(s) is it appropriate?

It's a style that you might like to try imitating. You could try creating a very 'girly' girl, whose shallow interests are limited to what's fashionable and her looks. Or a boy whose towering intellect renders him nauseatingly disdainful of his fellow pupils. Or a mother who is absorbed by trivia.

Imaginative writing – the dangers of poetry!

!Look out for

You need to incorporate the techniques you have learned from these short stories into your own narratives. Reading critically and analytically will enable you to write creatively and effectively.

Unless you have been commended for your poetic talents, avoid submitting poetry. It's a highly subjective art form that markers find difficult to assess. One of the major factors is length. Who is to say that a four-line poem is or is not a masterpiece? In other words, length alone cannot be an indication of quality. Write poetry by all means, but better not to submit it as part of your Folio.

Personal writing

Candidates who choose personal writing tend to do well. And there are very good reasons why: there isn't any particular form to personal writing the way that a short story has a form or a poem has a form. You can write personally in any way you wish – as a diary, as an essay, formally or informally.

Despite the freedom that personal writing gives you, there are certain requirements:

▶ you must demonstrate your ability to reflect on whatever experience you are writing about, and to express your thoughts and feelings

▶ you must pay attention to and not deviate from the rubric of the task set.

According to the marking instructions, to ensure a Grade 1:

▶ your essay should be well-crafted and stylish

▶ your essay should also be perceptive and reveal self-awareness (in other words, you should allow your personality to shine through)

▶ you should demonstrate an ability to achieve effects.

How to pull it off!

You may well ask what all the above means in practice. The following is by a candidate who set himself the following personal essay task:

'Myself
An entire dramatic company.'
The roles I play in life.

Note the aptness of the title:

Cast List

Shakespeare gives a man seven roles to play. But he's considerate; they come one by one, not all at once. They each have their little space of time allotted to them. Me – my roles contradict, my repertoire is vast. I can play them all at once or one after another; I can give you whole speeches extempore. 'All the world's a stage'; but the audience will gladly ignore you if you don't play your part. I won't play to an empty house, I won't be on my own. I can play a clown, a hero, a lover, a wise man, a fool. I can sing and jig, I can sermonise and weep, I can tell funny stories and have you laughing at me, with me, against me, for me. I know my part so well that I believe it implicitly – a keen student of the Method, I, I get inside the skin of every role.

The Intellectual, perhaps my greatest part. I could almost say that I created this in the original production. Certainly I gave the premiere in my area. Note the attention to detail – the copy of Brecht hidden not too ostentatiously in the, over-large, pile of books, the Lyceum Theatre Club card displayed when I open my wallet, the stoop, the precise but pensive mannerisms. Also note the turns of phrase – the quotations, the tendency to say 'I think' after facts I know are right (Oh he's so modest, he knows that but he doesn't want to show it). My greatest role – but one only to be performed before invited audiences. The audience must be educated to understand the nuances – if they don't recognise an intellectual, if they can't pick up the references, the whole effect is lost. Still, I'm proud of it.

continued

The reference to Shakespeare and *As You Like It* is not only fitting, it is also clever in that it reveals that the author has read widely! The use of allusion (references to literary texts) is highly commendable because it demonstrates knowledge and your ability to create effects – you let the reference make the point for you.

Throughout, the candidate adopts an endearing self-deprecatory stance, where he almost apologises for aspects of his personality, yet at the same time recognises his abilities. It's very clever, a mixture of what is almost conceit with a touch of charming diffidence. And although this is a personal essay, what he writes is well-crafted and certainly stylish, and it reveals self-awareness.

After dealing with the Intellectual, he goes on to deal with the other roles he plays, all of which emerge as aspects of his own personality: the Clown, the Lover, the Common Man, the Philosopher, the Writer. But throughout, he subtly conveys the idea that they are none of them quite real, they are inventions. Look what he says about the philosopher:

He thinks deeply about the world's problems – he's taciturn but he's obviously wise and thoughtful. For this role I did careful research. The facial expression is decidedly Christ-like. I saw how the wisest expression is one with hollow cheeks: Keats had it, so did Byron. I learnt just how how one can comfortably suck them in, making the cheek-bones more prominent. I learnt just how to make myself look unwell: a touch of illness is always good in a philosopher. This part works best at home; in public it's a bit embarrassing and not at all impressive. It's quite good for the Lover, though.

This is very clever – he claims that he (the candidate) is carefully contriving an image for the world, but, of course, this is a writer carefully crafting a narrator, who in turn is presenting an image of himself for the reader. Look at his use of the third person when he is actually talking about himself – an ability to dissociate himself from the author (the candidate) and see the narrator (the 'I' of the story) quite objectively. He slips easily between the third and first persons: 'He thinks deeply about the world's problems – he's taciturn but he's obviously wise and thoughtful. For this role I did careful research'. The use of both the 'he' and the 'I' helps portray the idea that these roles are inventions. Such skill with language is commendable.

The references to the Romantic poets – Keats and Byron – again reveals knowledge, even although it may all be contrived for effect. The last throwaway sentence is particularly effective.

But look how it ends:

And what's my role just now? A combination of them all? Or is the writer another of them, are these really my thoughts here? I think they are, but I'm an imperfect judge. They may be the thoughts of a character I've created – the best drama is the one we write for ourselves. My people dance around my brain; when I'm writing they take turns who shall guide the pen, who shall wave their hands in front of my eyes.

There must come a time when I can play myself. It's not come for years; it may never come. And can I do it anyway? I've been acting for ten or eleven years now. It becomes a habit. When I take all my make-up off, drop my accent, stop the character walk, what will be left? I'm frightened. I don't know what's there.

Here we have the reflection, the perceptive self-awareness, the place where the candidate's personality shines through, the hallmarks of the very best essays.

The art of telling a story

When you relate some event that took place in school either to your parents or to a friend who was absent, do you give an entirely blow-by-blow account or do you alter it, exaggerating here, editing there, embellishing, perhaps, the part that you played? Do you make yourself out to have been slightly more heroic than you were, delivering a much more cutting, wittier line than you actually did? Of course you alter stories – we all do.

The very presence of an audience makes us react, makes us want to entertain, enthral, shock our listeners. The process is exactly the same with readers. The most wonderfully satisfying aspect about writing is that we get the time to invent and craft the very best line, the wittiest remark, the most revengeful comment, the most acidic, vitriolic rebuke, all of which satisfy us as writers and amuse the reader. Writing allows us to shape stories and mould ourselves into the person we sometimes aspire to be. It lets us come to terms with the complexity of human experience.

Literature and reading

Standard Grade refers to literature as 'reading', a term which can be easily confused with *close* reading. We will therefore use the term literature as much as possible, and when we do use the term 'reading' it will be with reference to the demands of the Folio.

Although in this section we are going to be examining how you set about writing the three 'reading' pieces for your Folio, we are first of all going to look at *all* the stages you have to go through in the study of literature before you come to put pen to paper or fingers to a keyboard.

The deadline for the submission of Folios is the end of March of the year that you sit your examination, but your teacher will want your final Folio to be handed in by the end of February to ensure that the March deadline is met. That means that you have from August to the following February to complete all five pieces (two writing and three reading) – about six months.

This chapter will cover the two essential elements you need for your Reading Folio work: literature study skills and literature essay-writing skills.

Literature study skills

Since Standard Grade does not have set or even specified texts, there is little point in investigating in detail any individual texts here. But what we can do is examine closely *how you should approach* whatever text your teacher is studying with you in class, though we will look at parts of some texts as examples. We'll look at:

▶ *how* to approach the text in the first place

▶ *how* to analyse it

▶ *how* to prepare for writing a critical evaluation of it.

After all that, we'll consider carefully all that is involved in a critical evaluation and how to go about writing one.

The literature course

Literature can be classified into three genres: drama, prose, and poetry. Prose can be further sub-divided into prose fiction and prose non-fiction. Prose fiction can comprise novels and short stories. In addition, the study of media can also be part of your course.

You will have already studied plays, novels, short stories, poetry and you will therefore be acquainted with terms such as theme, structure, characterisation, setting, symbolism, plot, stage instructions, rhyme schemes, even rhythm.

But *how* should we approach works of literature? What part do all these terms play in our study of drama or fiction or poetry?

A useful approach!

You must have experienced the situation where your teacher reads a poem to the class, then asks for a reaction: all heads down, no-one wanting to catch her eye just in case, no-one quite sure what to say. Well, there's a way out of this situation so that you never need to be speechless again. The following is a framework of questions that you can have in your head, the answer to any one of which will at least allow you to make some meaningful comment. Next time a teacher asks for your opinion on a text, run through these questions:

 (i) What is the text about?

 (ii) What techniques has the author used (to portray what it's about)?

(iii) How do these techniques actually contribute (to what it's about)?

What is the text about?

Let's look at (i): and let's be clear right at the beginning that the answer to the question: 'What is the text about?' is not a retelling of the plot. The answer to (i) is **theme**. Other words for theme are issues, or concerns, or key ideas. It's best if you can state the theme in as few words as possible. For example, you can give the answer: 'I think the theme of *An Inspector Calls* is the importance of *social responsibility*.'

You'll be delighted to know that actually there are only three themes that writers concern themselves with – birth, marriage, and death. Let's take that a bit further and look at these three themes one by one:

Birth

Obviously a birth in any literary work can have an impact on relationships, but let's take birth in its widest context: the fact that we are born raises questions such as, Why am I here? What about my future? What will become of me? What are my ambitions? What is life about? Why am I me and not someone else? Are we the only inhabited place in the Universe? Is there a God? Has life a purpose or is it all one cruel accident?

Marriage

Let's take 'marriage' to cover all relationships and the questions that arise from them: explorations of our relationships with parents, with friends, with members of the opposite sex, with members of the same sex, with authority all of which give rise to themes such as jealousy, betrayal, fulfilment, resentment, revenge, love, sex.

continued

Death

Death is, of course, an important part of tragedy, since through death comes resolution, and the death of the protagonist (see drama) can often be redemptive; but by 'death' we also mean the thoughts and questions that arise towards the end of someone's life: questions such as, Why was I here? What have I done with my life? Have I achieved what I hoped when I was young? Has life passed me by? Is there a God? Is there life after death? What is death? What do I do with the years that remain, how do I want to spend them?

What techniques has the author used (to portray what it's about)?

The answer to the question 'What techniques has the author used?' is important since your critical examination has to deal with techniques by which the theme has been portrayed or conveyed: techniques (as appropriate) such as structure, characterisation, setting, symbolism, plot, stage instructions, rhyme schemes, rhythm, alliteration, assonance, and so on.

How do these techniques actually contribute (to what it's about)?

The answer to the question 'How do these techniques actually contribute?' is the **critical analysis, practical criticism**, or **textual analysis**. The examination of *how* the particular technique contributes to the portrayal of theme is the basis of a critical evaluation. It's not enough for you to be able to identify a technique, you *must* be able to analyse *how* that technique makes the contribution that it does to the theme. It is not enough, for example, to be able to say, 'Note the alliteration' or even 'Note the effect of the alliteration', you must also be able to analyse *how* the alliteration contributes to the overall point that is being made or the theme that is being explored.

When it comes to the individual genre, we will look at the appropriate techniques, such as stage instructions for drama and rhyme scheme for poetry.

Prose fiction

Let's begin with prose fiction. You've read the novel and the first thing you have to think about is theme. At this stage, it is important to remember that our initial idea of theme will get revised, developed, and most probably extended in the light of our analysis of the techniques.

So: what are the most important aspects of the novel? First and foremost is theme. All novels (and short stories) explore some facet of the human condition. Then there are the techniques: structure, narrative voice, characterisation (including names), setting, plot, symbolism We'll take each in turn:

Structure

As we have already discussed, structure has to do with time – *beginning-middle-end* or *middle-beginning-end* or even *beginning-flashback to time prior to the beginning-middle-more flashback-end*.

A novel such as Scott Fitzgerald's *The Great Gatsby*, for example, is almost entirely flashback, but within the flashback there are other several smaller flashbacks that go back to a time long before the novel actually begins and help to establish Gatsby's character.

That's also a technique used by John Steinbeck in *Of Mice and Men*, where throughout the beginning of the narrative we get several flashbacks that increasingly explain the present situation.

There is also the time when the novel is set and the timescale over which it takes place. J D Salinger's *Catcher in the Rye* is set in New York over a four-day period – and that is integral to the story which covers the period from when Holden Caulfield (the main character) is expelled from school until he is accepted into a mental institution to help in his recovery from the breakdown which takes place throughout the four-day period. Since the novel is about adolescent angst, exploring Caulfield's difficulties in facing adult responsibilities and behaviour, the short timescale contributes intensely to all that Caulfield is experiencing. Again, flashback is an important feature of this structure since it helps explain what led up to his breakdown.

Look out for

Flashback is a very useful technique whereby aspects of plot and character can be effectively explained to the reader.

Now try this

For any chosen novel, you should be able to work out:

▶ the way your chosen novel is structured in time

▶ the period in which it is set

▶ the timescale over which it takes place.

Be sure that you can then relate your findings to the overall theme(s) of the novel.

Narrative voice

The person who writes a novel or a short story is the **author**: he is the person who sits at the keyboard taking decisions about theme, character, setting, style and so on. The author creates a **narrator** or **narrative voice**. Every time you write yourself, you create a narrative voice which isn't always your own. In fact, it's fairly likely that it won't be your own.

There are various ways in which the author can create a narrative voice:

▶ omniscient narration

▶ first person narration

▶ third person narration

▶ multiple narration

▶ stream of consciousness.

Look out for

The narrator (or narrative voice) should not be confused with the author!

Omniscient narration

In **omniscient narration**, the story is told by a narrator who is all-knowing: he or she knows everything about all the characters and is able to switch from setting to setting. *Of Mice and Men* by John Steinbeck is an excellent example of the use of the omniscient narrator, as you can tell by this short extract:

> *"Lennie!" he said sharply. "Lennie, for God' sakes don't drink so much." Lennie continued to snort into the pool. The small man leaned over him and shook him by the shoulder. "Lennie. You gonna be sick like you was last night."*
>
> *Lennie dipped his whole head under, hat and all, and then he sat up on the bank and his hat dripped on his blue coat and ran down his back. "Tha's good," he said. You drink some, George. You take a good big drink." He smiled happily.*
>
> *George unslung his bindle and dropped it gently on the bank. "I ain't sure it's good water," he said. "Looks kinda scummy."*

The narrator here is like a camera, recording everything to be seen and heard. The narrator at no point intrudes, he simply records. Even 'He smiled happily' is observation. Note the tiny flashback: 'You gonna be sick *like you was last night*', giving us some character information.

First person narration

In **first person narration**, the story is told by one of the characters using the first person pronoun, I. The benefit of this kind of narration is that the reader gets to know and usually like the narrator but the problem is that the reader can only get to know the other characters from the narrator's viewpoint. Moreover, the narrator has to be present at all times or have information given to him or her by a third party, and even then we have only the narrator's word for it! There is no real objectivity in a novel narrated in the first person. Here is an extract from the opening of *The Buddha of Suburbia* by Hanif Kureishi.

> *My name is Karim Amir, and I am an Englishman born and bred, almost. I am often considered to be a funny kind of Englishman, a new breed as it were, having emerged*

Narrative voice – continued

from two old histories. But I don't care – Englishman that I am (though not proud of it), from the South London suburbs and going somewhere. Perhaps it is the odd mixture of continents and blood, of here and there, of belonging and not, that makes me restless and easily bored. Or perhaps it was being brought up in the suburbs that did it. Anyway, why search the inner room when it's enough to say that I was looking for trouble, any kind of movement, action and sexual interest I could find, because things so gloomy, so slow and heavy, in our family, I don't know why. Quite frankly, it was all getting me down and I was ready for anything.

Then one day everything changed. In the morning things were one way and by bedtime another. I was seventeen.

On this day my father hurried home from work not in a gloomy mood. His mood was high, for him. I could smell the train on him as he put his briefcase away behind the front door and took off his raincoat, chucking it over the bottom of the banisters. He grabbed my fleeing little brother, Allie, and kissed him; he kissed my mother and me with enthusiasm, as if we'd recently been rescued from an earthquake. More normally, he handed Mum his supper: a packet of kebabs and chapattis so greasy their wrapping paper had disintegrated. Next, instead of flopping into a chair to watch the television news and wait for Mum to put the warmed-up food on the table, he went into their bedroom, which was downstairs next to the living room. he quickly stripped to his vest and underpants.

Instantly, Karim Amir introduces himself, and we are in no doubt that he is the narrator: '**My** name is Karim Amir, and **I** am an Englishman, born and bred, almost.' It is as though we are meeting him for the first time, that he is there in front of us, an effect reinforced by the use of the present tense. There is then a switch to the past tense after the third sentence, signalling the use of flashback and the story itself.

The first sentence instantly attracts our attention and engages our interest by the positioning of 'almost' at the very end. Many of the subsequent details support the idea of his Britishness while others, particularly the behaviour of his father, suggest his Indian ethnicity. Try to identify these details and classify them accordingly.

What is also interesting is the language used by the author to create the character of Karim. We are persuaded that it is a 17 year-old boy speaking directly to us, yet it is actually very difficult to create the language of the spoken word in prose. We don't speak in sentences. Try to imagine a transcript conversation between you and a friend: it would be full of 'ums' and 'ers' and hesitations, unfinished sentences, sentence changes in the course of forming them. But Kureishi, the author behind Karim Amir, manipulates the language in such a way that, although it is not a true reflection of how a teenage boy would actually speak, it does 'sound' like it. What techniques does he use to achieve this effect? What does he say that persuades us that he is a 17 year-old, modern teenager?

Notice also the use of long sentences, particularly the penultimate (second last) sentence of the first paragraph. The use of phrases inserted into the sentence creates the impression that he is thinking as he is speaking. Note also the importance of the second paragraph, which has a pivotal role in the structure: it marks the change that is to come and signals that it happens very quickly.

Do we like the boy? If so, what aspects of what he says endear us to him? If not, why not? What aspects of the text make us want to read on? Try to base your answer on the language used.

continued

Third person narration

In **third person narration**, the story is being told in the third person, but unlike omniscient narration, the focus is restricted to one character. Many short stories use this method of narration. To illustrate the point, let's examine another extract from *Uneasy Homecoming* by Will Jenkins:

There was a soft sound at the back door. It squeaked.

Connie stood rigid. The clicking of the dial would tell everything. She could not conceivably summon help.

There was the soft whisper of a foot on the kitchen linoleum. Connie's hands closed convulsively. The only thought that came to her now was that she must breathe quietly.

There was a grey glow somewhere. The figure in the kitchen was throwing a torch beam on the floor. Then it halted, waiting. He knew that she was hiding somewhere in the house.

He went almost soundlessly into the living room. She saw the glow of the light there. Back into the kitchen. She heard him moving quietly – listening – toward the door through which she had come only a few seconds before to use the telephone.

He came through that door, within three feet of her. But when he was fully through the doorway she was behind him. Again he flashed the light downwards. But he did not think to look behind him. By just so much she was saved for the moment.

In the greyish light reflected from the floor she recognised him.

He went into the dining-room. He moved very quietly, but he bumped ever so slightly against a chair. The noise made her want to shriek. He was hunting her, and he knew that she was in the house, and he had to kill her. He had to get his loot and get away, and she must not be able to tell anything about him.

He was back in the kitchen again. He stood there, listening, and Connie was aware of a new and added emotion which came of her recognition of him. She felt that she would lie down at any instant and scream – because she knew him!

He came towards the door again, but he went up the stairs. They creaked under his weight. He must have reasoned cunningly that she would want to hide, because she was afraid. So he would go into the bedroom and look under the bed.

The focus is entirely on Connie. The only descriptions we are given are those of which Connie is aware. The sounds indicated in the very first sentence – 'There was a soft sound at the back door. It squeaked' – are the sounds that Connie hears. At no point in this extract, or in the whole short story – are we given any information about anyone else's thoughts or feelings. The effect of this type of narration is that the main character's thoughts, feelings, reactions are all intensified. And it keeps a short story focused.

Multiple narration

Multiple narration involves several narrators telling the story. The perfect example of multiple narration is *Dracula* by Bram Stoker, where there are several narrators and types of narration, such as telegrams and newspaper articles. The benefit is that the reader can put together for him or herself an objective view of events.

Also, *Stone Cold* by Robert Swindells has an interesting two-narrator structure: the character, Shelter, the enemy of the street people, relates his narrative as he hunts down the homeless, while alternative chapters are narrated by Link, the hero.

Stream of consciousness

It is unlikely that you will come across a novel narrated by **streams of consciousness** in your Standard Grade course. The narration attempts to imitate a character's thoughts as he or she thinks them.

Characterisation and plot

Character in fiction can be established in a number of ways. Let's look at the very beginning of *Emma* by Jane Austen:

Emma Woodhouse, handsome, clever, and rich, with a comfortable home and happy disposition, seemed to unite some of the best blessings of existence; and had lived nearly twenty-one years in the world with very little to distress or vex her.

She was the youngest of the two daughters of a most affectionate, indulgent father, and had, in consequence of her sister's marriage, been mistress of his house from a very early period. Her mother had died too long ago for her to have more than an indistinct remembrance of her caresses, and her place had been supplied by an excellent woman as governess, who had fallen little short of a mother in affection.

Sixteen years had Miss Taylor been in Mr. Woodhouse's family, less as a governess than a friend, very fond of both daughters, but particularly of Emma. Between them it was more the intimacy of sisters. Even before Miss Taylor had ceased to hold the nominal office of governess, the mildness of her temper had hardly allowed her to impose any restraint; and the shadow of authority being now long passed away, they had been living together as friend and friend very mutually attached, and Emma doing just what she liked; highly esteeming Miss Taylor's judgment, but directed chiefly by her own.

The real evils indeed of Emma's situation were the power of having rather too much her own way, and a disposition to think a little too well of herself; these were the disadvantages which threatened alloy to her many enjoyments. The danger, however, was at present so unperceived, that they did not by any means rank as misfortunes with her.

Sorrow came—a gentle sorrow—but not at all in the shape of any disagreeable consciousness.—Miss Taylor married. It was Miss Taylor's loss which first brought grief. It was on the wedding-day of this beloved friend that Emma first sat in mournful thought of any continuance. The wedding over and the bride-people gone, her father and herself were left to dine together, with no prospect of a third to cheer a long evening. Her father

continued

composed himself to sleep after dinner, as usual, and she had then only to sit and think of what she had lost.

Look how much we learn about Emma from the first sentence – a beautifully crafted one sentence paragraph, which so economically conveys many aspects of Emma's personality, set out in climactic order: she is handsome, clever, and rich. She has everything going for her with very little to distress or vex her. From that phrase alone we can undoubtedly anticipate the plot: she is going to be distressed and vexed!

Try listing what we get to know about Emma from the second paragraph. Look at the sequencing – we have to be told all about Miss Taylor in order to understand how Emma feels. What does highly esteeming Miss Taylor's judgement, but directed chiefly by her own suggest about Emma? Look how the next paragraph develops that characteristic. What is the sorrow that is referred to in the final paragraph? Look at the effect of the short sentence: 'Miss Taylor married' – short, sharp, and highly dramatic.

Again the reader is almost being set up for the plot: someone is going to replace Miss Taylor and Emma is going to get her own way! Thus in 5 short paragraphs right at the very opening of the novel we learn about Emma and have some idea of the plot. By these means, the opening raises our expectations; the remainder of the novel fulfils and satisfies them.

Setting and symbolism

Setting in time and place is hugely important in any novel. The time when a novel is written and when it is set often provide important contexts that can help the reader understand some of its themes. *Lord of the Flies* by William Golding, for example, was written in 1954, when, at the height of the Cold War, the threat of annihilation by nuclear holocaust was very real. Golding sets the novel during a nuclear war, from which a group of boys have been evacuated but have crash landed on a tropical island.

Here is the opening of the novel:

The boy with fair hair lowered himself down the last few feet of rock and began to pick his way toward the lagoon. Though he had taken off his school sweater and trailed it now from one hand, his grey shirt stuck to him and his hair was plastered to his forehead. All round him the long scar smashed into the jungle was a bath of heat. He was clambering heavily among the creepers and broken trunks when a bird, a vision of red and yellow, flashed upwards with a witchlike cry; and this cry was echoed by another.

"Hi!" it said. "Wait a minute!"

The undergrowth at the side of the scar was shaken and a multitude of raindrops fell pattering.

"Wait a minute," the voice said. "I got caught up."

The fair boy stopped and jerked his stockings with an automatic gesture that made the jungle seem for a moment like the Home Counties.

Setting and symbolism – continued

The voice spoke again. "I can't hardly move with all these creeper things."

The owner of the voice came backing out of the undergrowth so that twigs scratched on a greasy wind-breaker. The naked crooks of his knees were plump, caught and scratched by thorns. He bent down, removed the thorns carefully, and turned around. He was shorter than the fair boy and very fat. He came forward, searching out safe lodgments for his feet, and then looked up through thick spectacles.

"Where's the man with the megaphone?"

The fair boy shook his head. "This is an island. At least I think it's an island. That's a reef out in the sea. Perhaps there aren't any grownups anywhere."

The fat boy looked startled.

Notice that characterisation is also established in the above extract, but we will focus on setting and symbolism. The two are often connected: setting can be symbolic, as is the case here. The word choice 'lagoon', 'jungle', 'creepers' in the opening paragraph establish the fact that the setting is tropical and by the end of the extract we are fairly sure it is an island. A tropical island – the symbol of paradise! But, on the other hand, the word choice 'scar' (suggestion of injury, ugliness), 'smashed' (violence), 'his grey shirt stuck to him' (sweat plus the ugliness of the word stuck), 'his hair was plastered to his forehead' (sweat reinforced), 'clambering heavily' (difficulty in moving), 'a vision of red and yellow' (violent colours), 'witch-like cry' (evil, ugliness) all convey the possibility that all is not well, that this could be the antithesis of paradise – hell on earth.

The term 'Home Counties' (the counties surrounding London, populated largely by the middle classes) lets us know the fair boy is English and possibly public school, whereas the 'greasy wind-cheater' suggests that the other boy isn't from the same social class. He is also shorter than the fair boy and very fat. He wears 'thick spectacles'. The clothes, the gestures, the size of both boys are all symbolic, representing aspects of humanity.

We are left at the end of the extract wondering why the possibility of the lack of grown-ups startles the fat boy. Clearly something is going to go terribly wrong in this island 'paradise'. You should read the book.

Prose non-fiction

The danger in dealing with biography and autobiography, and with travel writing and journalism is that you get too involved with the content and not sufficiently involved in the ways in which the author has created the effects. When dealing with prose non-fiction try to concentrate on *how* the author has engaged your interest, what makes the book appealing, the effects of structure and linguistic skills. With prose non-fiction you have to focus very clearly on structure and language.

Drama

The essence of all drama is conflict. If you remember that, you won't go far wrong in your study of your chosen play. Think of any drama you watch on television – *The Bill*, *Coronation Street*, *Eastenders*, *Hollyoaks*, or any film you have seen recently – and all of them involve conflict.

There are two kinds of conflict. In less subtle dramas, the conflict is **external** and obvious: goodies-vs-baddies, cops-vs-robbers, men-vs-women, age-vs-youth. It's the same with Shakespeare – his plays involve external conflict, but what makes them really interesting is that they also involve **internal conflict**.

Let's call the main character in any drama the **protagonist**. The word, as with so many technical terms in literature, is Greek and originally meant the first actor. Today the word has taken on connotations of hero, and we will use it to mean the agent for good. Can you work out who is the protagonist in the play you are studying?

The character who represents the forces of evil we will call the **antagonist**. He or she is the person opposing the protagonist. For example, Othello, in the play of the same name, is the protagonist and Iago is the antagonist. In *Romeo and Juliet*, the protagonists are Romeo and Juliet themselves, and although Tybalt might be regarded as the antagonist, what opposes the lovers are antagonistic forces, such as the hatred between the two families. The antagonist may well be a character, but there could also be antagonistic forces which have more to do with the setting – physical, cultural, societal – than an individual.

But it is internal conflict which makes drama so interesting: when the protagonist has within him or her antagonistic forces, struggling against some aspect of himself or herself. Shakespeare's tragic heroes – Hamlet, Othello, and King Lear – all suffer from internal conflict as well as being in conflict with antagonists. The exception, of course, is Macbeth, who is the main character but is an **anti-hero**. But even he suffers from internal conflict, as he struggles, towards the end of the play, with the emptiness of his existence:

Life's but a walking shadow, a poor player
That struts and frets his hour upon the stage
And then is heard no more. It is a tale
Told by an idiot, full of sound and fury,
Signifying nothing.

Stage instructions

The importance of stage instructions, especially in modern drama, cannot be over-emphasised. It's interesting to compare the instructions in a Shakespeare play such as *Macbeth*, first performed in the early 1600s with a fairly modern play, such as *The Long and the Short and the Tall* by Willis Hall, first performed in 1958.

Contrasting examples

Let's look first of all at *Macbeth*. The following is the beginning of the murder scene – the murder of King Duncan takes place offstage. Note how few stage instructions there are – it's a room in Macbeth's castle, but how is it furnished, what's its purpose, from where does Macbeth enter?

Act 2 Scene 2

Macbeth's castle, near Duncan's room.

Enter Lady Macbeth

LADY MACBETH

That which hath made them drunk hath made me bold;
What hath quench'd them hath given me fire.

[*an owl shrieks*]

Hark! Peace!
It was the owl that shriek'd, the fatal bellman,
Which gives the stern'st good–night. He is about it:
The doors are open; and the surfeited grooms
Do mock their charge with snores: I have drugg'd their possets,
That death and nature do contend about them,
Whether they live or die.

In total contrast, the stage instruction for *The Long and the Short and the Tall* is lengthy, as are most stage instructions for modern plays. Note how specific it is – *Late afternoon*. And every detail is given: *all that remains is a rickety table and two chairs, Centre Stage, and a form, Right*. Note the specificity of the sound effects and the sheer detail of the moves the actors have to make.

Time: Late afternoon.

The curtain rises on the wooden-walled, palm-thatched, dingy interior of a deserted store-hut in the Malayan jungle. The hut is set back a few hundred yards from a tin mine which is now deserted. There is a door in the rear wall with windows on either side looking out onto the veranda and jungle beyond. The hut has been stripped of anything of value by the mine-workers before they fled – all that remains is a rickety table and two chairs, Centre Stage, and form, Right. We hear a short burst of gunfire in the distance – and then silence.
A pause and then we hear the chirruping of crickets and the song of the bird in the jungle. A figure appears in the Left Hand window, looks cautiously inside and ducks away. A moment later the door is kicked open and JOHNSTONE stands framed in the doorway, holding a sten at his hip. When the door was kicked open the crickets and the bird ceased their song. JOHNSTONE glances around the room

continued

and, finding it unoccupied, makes a hand signal from the veranda.
JOHNSTONE *returns into the room and is joined by* MITCHEM, *who also carries a sten.*

Why the difference? Is it because playwrights know that their plays are likely to be read and that therefore the details are for a reader's benefit and not an actor's or a director's? Or is it because playwrights do not want directors and / or actors to take liberties with their scripts? Whatever the reason, you should pay attention to what is said because you can make reference to the stage instructions in your essays.

Characterisation

It is important to remember that we get to know characters in a play by stage instructions, by their actions, by what they say, or by what other characters say about them.

If you read the extract below, you can see that the characters in *The Long and the Short and the Tall* are all tired and *dishevelled*. Mitchem *slams* the door – suggesting what? What do Bamforth's actions suggest about him? What does his *studied unconcern* suggest about his attitude to Johnstone, his superior; and therefore does that look suggest anything about his attitude to authority? Is there anything else in the stage instructions which confirms your opinion about Bamforth?

JOHNSTONE (*shifts his hat to the back of his head and places his sten on the table*): All Clear. Stinks like something's dead.

MITCHEM (*placing his sten beside* JOHNSTONE's): It'll do. To be going on with. (*He crosses to the door and motions to the rest of the patrol.*) Come on, then! Let's have you!… Move it! Move!

One by one the members of the patrol double into the room. With the exception of WHITAKER, *who carries the radio transmitter/receiver on his back, the men are armed with rifles.*

SMITH *carries* WHITAKER's *rifle. They are tired and dishevelled.*

JOHNSTONE: Move yourselves! Gillo! Lacas!

As the last member of the patrol enters the room MITCHEM *slams the door. The men stack their rifles in a corner and sit gratefully on the table.* WHITAKER *takes off the 'set' and sets it up on the table.* BAMFORTH *shrugs off his pack, places it as a pillow on the form, and makes himself comfortable.*

JOHNSTONE: How long are we here for?

MITCHEM (*glances at his watch*): Half an hour or so, and then we'll push off back. Better mount a guard. Two men on stag. Fifteen minute shifts.

JOHNSTONE: Right … (*He notices* BAMFORTH *who is now fully stretched out.*) Bamforth! … Bamforth!

BAMFORTH (*raises himself with studied unconcern*): You want me, Corp?

JOHNSTONE: Get on your feet, lad!

Stage instructions – continued

BAMFORTH: What's up?

JOHNSTONE: I said 'move'! (*BAMFORTH pulls himself slowly to his feet*) You think you're on holiday? Get your pack on!

BAMFORTH: You going to inspect us, Corp?

JOHNSTONE: Don't give me any of your mouth. Get your pack on! Smartish! Next time keep it on till you hear different.

BAMFORTH (*heaves his pack on to one shoulder*): All right! O.K. All right.

JOHNSTONE: Right on!

BAMFORTH *glances across at* MITCHEM.

MITCHEM: You heard what he said.

BAMFORTH (*struggles the pack on to both shoulders. He speaks under his breath*): Nit!

There is a pause. JOHNSTONE *crosses to face* BAMFORTH.

JOHNSTONE: What was that?

BAMFORTH: Me. I only coughed.

MITCHEM: O.K., Bamforth. Just watch it, son.

In this short piece of dialogue and stage instructions, a surprising amount is established: the play is set in the Malayan jungle; the patrol are exhausted; there is considerable tension between Bamforth and Johnstone.

When you are writing about the characters in any play you have studied, you have to remember that they aren't real. They are the presentations of the playwright's imagination, and they are there to enable him or her to portray the theme.

That means that when we come to analyse them we have to go by the text. We have to examine closely what is said in the stage instructions and in the dialogue. You can say, for example, that Johnstone takes his responsibilities seriously or that he has an overinflated sense of his own importance as a corporal – *but*, in order to support your opinion, you have to go to the text for evidence.

Now try this

By close reference to the text, note:

▶ your impression of Johnstone

▶ your impression of Bamforth

▶ your impression of Mitchem

▶ your impression of the relationship among all three of them.

Now examine carefully, in whatever play you are studying, the ways in which the characters and their relationships are established.

Setting

Setting is as integral a part of any drama as the characterisation, and is important in order to help present the theme. It is the interaction between the setting (time and place) and character that can make the most effective contribution to theme.

As an example, let's have a look at the setting in *An Inspector Calls* by J B Priestley. The play was first produced in October 1946 but is set in the spring of 1912, which means that Priestley is able to make reference with hindsight to events between these dates – Arthur Birling, for example, naively praises the technological wonder of the 'unsinkable' *RMS Titanic*, which of course sank on its maiden voyage on 15 April 1912.

Such a retrospective setting in time also allows Priestley to present other examples of Birling's misguided optimism: he comments for example that 'in twenty or thirty years' time – let's say in 1940 … There'll be peace and prosperity and rapid progress everywhere'. By 1940, as we all know, the world had been plunged into the most devastating of world wars. It is Priestley's use of the setting and time that allows him to present Birling's monumental arrogance and stupidity.

The actual physical setting is *the dining room of a fairly large suburban house* which belongs to a *prosperous manufacturer*. It is furnished to create a *heavily comfortable* effect but not one which is *cosy and homelike*. The word *suburban* has pejorative connotations, suggesting attitudes that are dull, conventional, narrow-minded, pretentious, materialistic.

All this setting represents symbolically the self-made man. Clearly, to afford such a place, Birling has money, but it isn't inherited money. He has gained it from the profits of manufacturing. In other words he is *nouveau riche* and *arriviste*: it is what is sometimes referred to as 'new money': he has become wealthy without the 'right' breeding and background, which means he is slightly uncomfortable and insecure about his position in society. That's why he courts Sir George and Lady Croft, whose son, Gerald, is *very much the easy well-bred young man-about town*. Again note the sheer detail of the stage instructions.

The dining-room of a fairly large suburban house, belonging to a prosperous manufacturer. It has good solid furniture of the period. The general effect is substantial and heavily comfortable, but not cosy and homelike. (If a realistic set is used, then it should be swung back, as it was in the production at the New Theatre. By doing this, you can have the dining-table centre downstage during Act One, when it us needed there, and then swinging back, can reveal the fireplace, and by this time the dining-table and its chairs have moved well upstage. Producers who wish to avoid this tricky business, which involves two re-settings of the scene and some very accurate adjustments of the extra flats necessary, would be well advised to dispense with an ordinary realistic set, if only because the dining-table becomes a nuisance. The lighting should be pink and intimate until the INSPECTOR arrives, and then it should be brighter and harder.)

At rise of curtain, the four BIRLINGS and GERALD are seated at the table, with ARTHUR BIRLING at one end, his wife at the other, ERIC downstage, and SHEILA and GERALD seated upstage. EDNA, the parlourmaid, is just clearing the table, which has no cloth, of dessert plates and champagne glasses, etc., and then replacing them with decanter of port, cigar box and cigarettes. Port glasses are already on the table. All five are in evening dress of the period, the men in tails and white ties, not dinner jackets. ARTHUR BIRLING is a heavy-looking, rather portentous man in his middle fifties with fairly easy manners but rather provincial in his speech. His wife is about fifty, a rather cold woman and her husband's social superior. SHEILA is a pretty girl in her twenties, very pleased with life and rather excited. GERALD CROFT is an attractive chap about thirty, rather too manly to be a dandy but very much the easy well-bred young man-about-town. ERIC is in his early twenties, not quite at ease, half shy, half assertive. At the moment they have all had a good dinner, are celebrating a special occasion, and are pleased with themselves.

The setting suggests pomposity, complacency, self-satisfaction, pretentiousness, all of which, we can anticipate, will be harshly and dramatically punctured by events to come.

Now try this

Consider the play you are studying in class and in a few paragraphs indicate the extent to which setting is a contribution to theme.

Structure

Finally, let's say a word about the ways in which plays are put together. Of course it is difficult to generalise, but plays really have to be 'built' block by block. The other metaphor that is sometimes used is that of the tying of a knot. The opening scenes reveal the strands of rope, the middle scenes are the tying of the knot and the final scenes are the untying of the knot.

That's a bit simplistic, but you get the point. The word *dénouement* (the resolution brought about by the ending of the play), after all, is a French word which means *untying*. There tends at the beginning of any play to be a situation which, however stable it appears, has the potential for becoming unstable. Then there is introduced some catalyst which speeds up the impending instability – in the case of *An Inspector Calls*, it is the arrival of the Inspector that has the catalytic effect and causes considerable disintegration of the apparent stability of the family. In *The Long and the Short and the Tall* it is the capturing of the Japanese prisoner that contributes to the build-up in tension among the patrol. In *Macbeth*, it is the witches' prophecies that precipitate the tragedy.

The ending of a drama is also highly significant. The knot has to be untied, but there also needs to be an element of **redemption** – a deliverance from the worst aspects that unfolded. Often such redemption involves a sacrifice – in a tragedy it is the hero's death that makes way for a more stable and enduring moral order. *An Inspector Calls* isn't a tragedy as such – no-one dies – but there is some sacrifice: Sheila forgoes her forthcoming marriage. And undoubtedly the younger generation – Sheila and Eric – learn from what they have been put through by the Inspector, whereas the older generation – Mr and Mrs Birling – sink back into their complacency. The very ending of the play, however, leaves the audience finally satisfied.

Poetry

You will undoubtedly study a number and variety of poems throughout your Standard Grade course and many of you will want to write about a poem for your critical evaluation.

Remember what you know about the narrative voice

As with fiction, let's separate the author from the person narrating or reflecting on events in a poem. The 'I' in such a poem we will refer to as the **persona**. If nothing else, this stops us from regarding the poem as autobiographical. To view the poet as 'speaking' the poem is to view the poem in too narrow a way. Poems, like fiction and drama, have a universal appeal – greater than the story or the individual involved. All art – paintings, sculpture, music, fiction, drama, poetry – is, of course, about something particular, but at the same time it explores and reflects in a much wider and deeper way something significant about the human condition. You'll see that in this Thomas Hardy poem.

The Self-Unseeing

Here is the ancient floor,
Footworn and hollowed and thin,
Here was the former door,
Where the dead feet walked in.

She sat here in her chair,
Smiling into the fire,
He who played stood there
Bowing it higher and higher.

Childlike, I danced in a dream;
Blessings emblazoned that day,
Everything glowed with a gleam,
Yet we were looking away!

Where to start?

How do you go about analysing the poem? Let's make this easy: read the poem again, very carefully, then look carefully at the table set out below. There are listed in it a number of techniques that you should bear in mind when approaching any poem. You should use the table as a checklist.

	Technique	Explanation
1	Situation	What situation or experience seems to have given rise to the poem?
2	Structure and verse form	Is the poem in stanzas or verse paragraphs? If the poem is in verse paragraphs, comment on the use of the paragraph to convey the point being made. If in stanzas, is there a rhyme scheme, and, if so, how does the rhyme scheme support what the poem is about?
3	Word choice	What words does the poet use to establish atmosphere, mood, attitude?
4	Sentence structure	Are there long sentences, short sentences, and do the sentences fit the stanza form? Are there any lists and, if so, what effect is created by the lists? Is there use of climax? Is there a change in tense? Most poems are written in the present tense.
5	Punctuation	Watch for all aspects of punctuation and the ways in which punctuation clarifies and/or affects meaning.
6	Tone	By examination of word choice and sentence structure work out if the tone is serious, bitter, amusing, sarcastic, sad, happy, etcetera. You should always be able to justify tone by referring closely to the poem, its language and imagery.
7	Enjambement	Sometimes referred to as *run-on lines*, where the poet, using regular stanza form, nevertheless spills the sentence from one line onto the next. For example, in Larkin's *Ambulances*, he writes: *Far* *From the exchange of love to lie* Where the phrase *far from the exchange of love* has been artificially but deliberately split by the line ending in order to create surprise: we do not expect to read *from the exchange of love* after the word *Far*.
8	Symbols	Does the poet employ symbols – i.e., is the reference to summer a season reference only or is it a reference to, say, the summer of our lives?
9	Line endings	Does the poet deliberately use the line ending to special effect?
10	Contrast and oxymoron	Be aware of the technique of contrast – many poets use it very effectively. Look out for contrasting language, images or symbols. Also be aware of oxymoron – a device that draws attention to contradictory words, and therefore the contradictory ideas behind the words
11	Metaphor	Metaphor is a device of comparison. For example: *Kevin was a lion in the fight* – where a study of lion-like qualities will tell us how Kevin fought. To determine whether a metaphor is effective, ask yourself if the thing to which the main item is being compared is appropriate – if it is, the metaphor is effective.

continued

Where to start? – continued

	Technique	Explanation
12	**Synecdoche**	Synecdoche is a device of representation. It is where a part is used to represent the whole – 'The pen is mightier than the sword', where 'the pen' represents not just writing but taking a calm thought-out attitude to some problem and 'the sword' represents violence, hot-headedness. But synecdoche is also used where a writer wants to convey ideas about a scene by concentrating on a small part of it: vultures can be used to represent death.
13	**Alliteration**	Sound device. Does the poet employ alliteration in order to reflect or echo meaning? Does this contribute to the sound of the poem, and, if so, in what way(s)?
14	**Assonance**	Another sound device. Does the poet use the repetition of vowel sounds (long or short) in order to create special effects – and, if so, how does the repetition of the vowel sound contribute to this effect?
15	**Personification**	Does the poet attribute to inanimate objects the characteristics and emotions of human beings? For example, the bus which has the following notice on its destination board: *I'm sorry, I'm not in service*. How can a bus feel contrition? What is the effect of this personification?
16	**Climax or anti-climax**	The build up of ideas or language achieved by meaning or by rhythm and sound.
17	**Transferred epithet**	For example, in the lines from D H Lawrence: *I picked up a clumsy log* *And threw it at the water-trough with a clatter* Clearly, the log isn't clumsy – it's the thrower, but the author has transferred the word *clumsy* from the thrower to the log to draw attention to the clumsiness.
18	**Comment on the title**	What can you comment on the title and how does it relate to the rest of the poem?

Time to take another look…

Let's now approach Hardy's *The Self-Unseeing* with this checklist in front of us.

1 The situation seems to be that the persona has visited his old home and is recalling a childhood scene there. The opening word – 'Here' – indicates the present, the here and now, which, combined with the use of the present tense, strongly implies that he is in a room now looking back at a previous time – his childhood?

2 The poem is in three 4-line stanzas, with an *a b a b* rhyme scheme: this structure makes the poem seem straightforward, almost child-like, yet it is deceptively adult.

3 Words and phrases such as 'ancient floor', 'Here was the former door', 'She sat here in her chair',… 'He who played higher and higher' all suggest looking back – to a time when he was with his parents? Then the childlike seems to confirm that he is looking back as an adult on a family scene, except of course they are all dead now: 'Where the dead feet walked in'.

4 Each stanza is one sentence long, which helps confirm the tight structure of the poem.

Where to start? – continued

5 The semi-colon at the end of the first line of the last stanza has the effect of linking his dancing as a child with the perfection of the time. But the use of the exclamation at the end of the last line draws attention to its meaning, highlighting the forcefulness of the comment.

6 The tone is reflective and ever so regretful towards the end. There is the build-up to the last line – 'Yet we were looking away': he was not aware at the time of how much he enjoyed his childhood. The 'Yet' indicates the change in tone – 'yet', in this instance, is a conjunction which signals 'in spite of', or 'nevertheless'. Although 'Blessings emblazoned that day', nevertheless 'we children were looking away', we didn't notice or even note the happiness of the experience.

7 There is no enjambement – all the lines are end-stopped, which contributes to the intense 'poetic' feel to the poem.

8 Symbols are used here – and they are synecdochic in that the description of a part represents the whole. For example, 'dead feet walked in' is a synecdochic image for the dead person. And:

She sat here in her chair,
Smiling into the fire,

is a synecdochic image of his mother, and the smiling into the fire represents an image of cosiness and family bliss.

9 The last line of the last stanza comes as a kind of a shock and suddenly changes the whole poem and makes the reader re-assess what has been said.

10 Hardy uses contrast to explore the theme – the fact that human beings when they are young don't reflect on how happy, blissful, they are. There is a sense then in which childhood is lost because 'we were looking away'. The contrasts then are between the present and the past, the persona as an adult and as a child, the 'Blessings emblazoned that day' where 'everything glowed with a gleam' and the almost soulful regret of 'Yet we were looking away'.

11 There is more use of synecdoche in this poem than metaphor, though the metaphor in 'Blessings emblazoned' is effective because the blessings of the day are being compared to a decorative shield, with its connotations of protectiveness and colour, or to a colourful banner hoisted by way of celebration. The experience is joyous.

12 See symbols – No 8 above.

13 Note the alliteration of the **b** sound in the expression 'Blessings emblazoned': the percussive nature of the sound reinforces the celebratory connotations; and the alliterated **g** sound of 'glowed with a gleam' and the long vowels of the words 'glowed' and 'gleam' combine to create a very pleasant, warm, clean image, that could refer to the physical room or to the family unit within it.

14 See No 13 above.

15 There is no personification.

16 The climax is clear and comment has already been made on it. It's the build-up to the last line and then the climax, which makes the reader reconsider what has been said and reflect on the experience.

17 There are no examples of transferred epithet.

18 After considering the poem, then we can examine the title; *The Self-Unseeing*. In the light of the last line, what appears at first glance to be an obscure title suddenly becomes remarkably clear. The self is his childhood self, but at the time, he was unaware of the bliss and happiness with which he was surrounded – he was 'unseeing'.

The table of poetic techniques is not exclusive. It is intended as a guideline only. But it does have the merit of providing for you notes that you can use as a basis for a critical evaluation.

Literature essay writing skills

Now we can turn our minds to the writing of the three literature pieces that you have to submit for your Folio: and remember that two of the pieces have to be from more than one genre.

Let's look at what the GRC demand for Credit and General. There is much to note:

Credit	General
Displays a thorough familiarity with the text(s): this appears e.g. in the analysis of its main ideas and purposes and through detailed reference to relevant areas of content.	Displays an acceptable familiarity with the text(s): this appears in a statement of its main ideas and purposes and through reference to some relevant areas of content.
Shows an ability to relate significant detail to the overall context of the work(s) studied.	Shows some ability to relate detail to the overall context of the work(s) studied.
Gives a perceptive and developed account of what s/he has enjoyed in/gained from the text(s): this clearly conveys the sense of a genuine personal response and is substantiated by reference to pertinent features of the text(s).	Makes a reasonably developed statement about aspects of the text(s) which have affected him/her: this conveys the sense of a genuine personal response and is accompanied by some reference to pertinent features of the text(s).
Demonstrates awareness of technique by analysis, using critical terminology where appropriate: this appears in full and perceptive explication of stylistic devices substantiated by detailed reference to the text(s) and, where appropriate, apt quotation.	Identifies individual features of technique and explains their effects, using basic critical terminology where appropriate: this involves the brief explication of obvious stylistic devices and is accompanied by some reference to the text(s) and/or quotation.

All this means that, to attain a Credit, you have to:

▶ demonstrate that you have a thorough knowledge of the text both in your analysis and your references

▶ demonstrate that you can refer in significant detail in order to demonstrate how the theme(s) have been portrayed

▶ demonstrate your engagement with the text

▶ demonstrate that you can employ critical terminology, that you can explain how meaning is shaped by linguistic and stylistic devices; and that you can refer aptly to the text to support your ideas.

Furthermore:

Credit	General
Organises the response in such a way as to reflect, accurately, the purpose and nature of the assignment: this appears in an ability to select what is relevant in the text(s) and give due weight and prominence to what is important; the response is a substantial one but not normally exceeding 800 words.	Organises the response so as to take some account of the purpose and nature of the assignment: most of what is selected from the text(s) is relevant and adequate attention is given to what is important; the response is a reasonably extended one, probably between 300 and 600 words.

To attain a credit, then, you have also to be able to organise your response so that it is relevant to the task you have been set or you have set yourself. To achieve that you must:

- be able to select relevantly from the text;

- give due weight to what is important;

- write a substantial response, not normally exceeding 800 words.

You will show confidence, write accurately, reveal sensitivity to effects, use critical terminology with confidence and produce a coherent and cohesive essay.

You personal response to the work should not be a paragraph tagged on to the end, saying: 'By the way I really enjoyed that poem..'. Your personal response should be integral to your essay, revealed through your understanding and sensitive appreciation of effect.

A critical evaluation of The Self-Unseeing

Below is a critical evaluation of *The Self-Unseeing*. In it, we have tried to incorporate all that a Credit award demands. The task is:

Discuss the extent to which the setting of time and place are essential aspects of the theme.

Note the repetition of the task in the opening sentence.

In *The Self-Unseeing* by Thomas Hardy, the poet creates a very strong sense of setting in both time and place, both of which are essential aspects of his portrayal of the theme: that we are not always able, as a child, to recognise straightforward happiness and unalloyed joy.

In the poem, the persona seems to be showing someone his childhood home, a place that clearly conjures up happy memories. The use of the opening word *Here* instantly involves the reader in the setting since *Here* suggests both place and time. Also, Hardy's use of the present tense in his opening line gives an immediacy and present-ness to the poem. The feeling is very much of present place and present time. The combination, however, of *here* with *ancient floor* makes clear that the experience is recalling a time long past from the present.

As he turns to look at the door, he comments: *Here was the former door,* where the sudden switch to the past tense makes clear that he is indeed recalling a memory and reflecting on a past event. The use of place – e.g., his reference to the door – suggests a darker, sadder theme: he recalls that through this door *the dead feet walked in,* suggesting that the people who lived there are now dead. The reference to *She sat here in her chair, / Smiling into the fire* suggests by its intimacy and intense domesticity his mother and, presumably, that the person playing the violin is his father. The happy memory is clearly being recalled by the place – the revisiting of a childhood room, yet the *dead feet* reminds the reader that these people are no longer with the persona. This darker theme is perhaps hinted at early in the poem when Hardy talks about the floor being *hollowed* – as reference perhaps to the fact that this part of the house was used frequently and had become *footworn* and *thin*. But *hollowed* has other connotations of an emptiness in their lives and therefore hints at a more melancholy mood.

This poem, then, is not simply a poem recalling past joy, a reflection on the ways in which the narrator's childhood was spent in innocence and family bliss. The last verse provides that joyful reflection on his past childhood with its references to dancing in dreams and blessings being emblazoned. Attention is finally drawn to the second last line *Everything glowed with a gleam* where the alliteration of the *g* sound draws attention to the meanings of the words, and, combined with the pleasant sounding long vowels of *glow* and *gleam*, the homeliness and joyfulness of the occasion is reinforced. The line is, however, in the past tense – the *glow* and the *gleam* were then, not now.

continued

But perhaps the line that underscores this darker side to the poem is the last line: *Yet we were looking away!* The *Yet* provides the link to the rest of the poem, but it also introduces the new idea – that at that time they, the children, were unaware of the happiness that surrounded them. The word *we* certainly suggests the persona's siblings, since clearly the mother and father are not looking away at the time. There seems to be, then, a strong feeling of regret that they were unaware of the happiness of that time and the use of the exclamation mark at the end of the sentence reinforces that idea. Though there does seem to be an odd contradiction in that the persona was aware of the blessings and the glowing of events that day, yet at the same time he looked away. Underlining this verse seems to be the idea that when you are young you do not always appreciate joyful experiences – only when you are older and reflect on these experiences do you recognise them for what they were.

In his poem *The Self-Unseeing*, Hardy very skilfully uses both time and place to reflect on his childhood. The place – in the present – helps him recall the experience in the past. But what is interesting is that the reflection is not a naïve recollection of childhood innocence but a deep awareness that we do not appreciate the happiness of childhood until it is too late.

(710 words)

Let's recap what you have to do

It is vitally important to remember that whenever you are presented with a text – short story, novel, play, poem, film – you have first of all to ask yourself what that text is about. In other words identify theme.

Thereafter, in attempting to understand and evaluate how the author has portrayed that theme, keep the following techniques in mind:

1 Examine **narrative voice** – how the piece is told:

   (a) first, second, third person – consider the effect

   (b) if third, point of view – does it shift or centre on one character – consider the effect

   (c) use of dialogue and its purpose – to establish character, drive forward the narrative.

2 **Use of setting and time** – how are both established – and the effect of both. Look carefully, especially at the beginning of the piece. How are both setting and time related to theme?

3 **How atmosphere/mood/tone are established** – use of word choice, connotations of words, weather, physical things.

4 **Formality of the piece** – look carefully at the sentences – considerable subordination usually makes for a fairly formal piece, whereas short sentences with many phrases and non-finite verbs indicate informality. Look for variety in sentence structure – long sentence followed by short one usually has a dramatic effect. Also, look out for any change in tense and the effect created by the change.

5 Look out for any **alteration from normal word order** since that can create dramatic or emphatic effect – *It was still dark outside and cold* – normally that would read *It was still dark and cold outside*, but by altering the word order Golding draws attention to and stresses the fact that it is cold.

6 Also be aware of **punctuation** and how it is being used.

7 Examine **words and their connotations** throughout – but also look for use of symbols – weather, seasons, journeys, etc.

8 What **images** (especially **metaphor** and **synecdoche**) have been used – how significant and effective are they? Bear in mind that images are not always visual, but can be to do with hearing, touch, smell, and taste.

9 Look for **poetic** or **literary devices** – prose uses *alliteration, assonance, oxymoron, contrast, hyperbole, rhythm, climax, anti-climax, personification*, as well as poetry – look at modern advertising for the use of poetic devices!

10 Is there any **foreshadowing**: where the narrator by means of events or symbols suggests what is to come.

11 Use of **symbolism**: where an object or animal or action is used to represent the events of the narrative and/or the theme of the text.

   If you are writing about poetry, bear in mind these particular techniques, specific to poetry:

12 Follow all the points above – they apply equally to poetry, including narrative voice and focus, though, of course, the poem may not be a narrative one. Also be aware of stanza structure, rhyme scheme, enjambement, line length, line endings, positioning, rhythm, sound (devices such as alliteration, assonance, onomatopoeia).

It is vital to remember that all texts concern themes – what is the text about? All techniques help reveal and explore the themes.

The task itself

Success in your Folio literature pieces largely depends on the nature of the task. Try to ensure that your task directs you to a specific analysis of the text: you really want a task that will allow you to examine the techniques by which the theme of your chosen text is realised or portrayed. Your essay must be detailed, accurate, and precise. If you're vague, you're unlikely to do well.

When writing your Critical Evaluation, you must:

1 **Introduce the material effectively and concisely USING THE WORDING OF THE TASK** so that the marker or examiner knows instantly and unambiguously what you are doing.

2 **Structure your material appropriately** – ensuring that your answer will cover all aspects of the task.

3 **Make sure that paragraphs are linked**; make sure that ideas are linked and balanced – use terms such as *moreover, furthermore, however, on the one hand…on the other, not only… but also, although x is the case, y also is the case, nevertheless, accordingly.*

4 Make sure that you **refer back to the task in each paragraph** – this will ensure that you remain relevant; use words such as *since, thus, hence, clearly, similarly* at the beginning of the paragraph to help indicate that you are proving a case.

5 **Avoid the formula** *quotation + comment* – above all, avoid the formula *quotation, this shows that…* work all quotations into the very structure of your sentence unless they are long, then set them out separately, indented from the margin.

6 **Conclude appropriately** – *Thus…* or *Clearly, it can be seen that…* and then refer back to the task and make the conclusion short without introducing any new material.

7 **Produce a cohesive and a coherent piece of prose** – **cohesive** means that it has to be well-linked and **coherent** means that it must make sense by itself because it has been appropriately introduced and concluded.

Pay particular attention to number agreement, which is a problem in English: avoid if you can the modern tendency to use **their** for the singular, for example, in the British Telecom 1471 message – 'The caller withheld their number' – **caller** is singular and therefore the pronoun should be **his/her**. Words such as **no-one**, **none** and **anyone** are singular and take a singular verb: None of us *is* going to the party.

!Look out for

Furthermore, avoid all informalities such as abbreviations and/or contractions: no *isn't, wasn't doesn't, cannot, shan't*. Be formal at all times.

If you fail to submit the right pieces in your Folio, you could end up with no grade and therefore no overall grade for English! If in doubt, check with your teacher.

Media texts and imaginative responses

In addition to reading drama, prose and poetry, you could also choose to use a media text or compose an imaginative response as part of your Folio reading pieces.

Let's be clear about this! If you choose to do a media text or an imaginative response to literature, you have to choose your other critical examinations from more than one literary genre. That is, if you choose media or an imaginative response, your other two critical evaluations have to be from drama and prose, or drama and poetry, or prose and poetry. (See page 9).

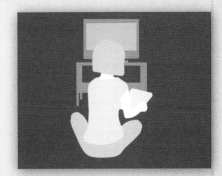

Media

Critical evaluations of media texts are becoming increasingly popular. The media text can be from film, radio, or television. But a strong word of warning: you should not attempt a critical evaluation of a media text if you have not been taught about film, radio, or television. Media is not an easy option where you can just chat about your favourite television programme.

Not only that, but for the purposes of the Folio media texts are defined as film, radio, or television programme or programmes. In other words, **print** media texts, such as newspaper articles, magazine advertisements, are **not** acceptable.

When it comes to studying film, you should follow the same procedure as a literary text: identify the theme, then look to the techniques used by the director to present or portray that theme.

You should be very aware of the techniques specific to film, radio and television. You need to know the effects of panning, tracking, close-ups, fading, long shots, long scenes, mise-en-scène, camera movement, the use of soundtrack to create mood, and so on.

The Internet can be a useful research tool for this area of study.

Imaginative response to literature

The other possibility is for you to produce an imaginative response to one of the pieces of literature that you have studied. These responses are less popular than they have been in previous years.

An imaginative response can be submitted as evidence of Writing, in which case it cannot be considered as evidence of Reading.

If it is submitted as evidence of Reading, then it must demonstrate a knowledge and understanding of the literary text – and **must**, if it is to attract a General or Credit grade, demonstrate a grasp of the mood and tone of the text of which it is a response as well as an understanding of one other technique, such as, where relevant, characterisation, setting, narrative voice,

imagery, symbolism, conflict, dialogue, contrast, stage instructions, rhythm, rhyme, word choice.

An example of an imaginative response might be a task which requires the opening of, say, *Catcher in the Rye*, rewritten with a female character as Holden Caulfield or recasting a scene from a play or novel in a different setting, either in time or place. What is important is that you demonstrate an understanding of theme and writer technique. You must, however, resist any temptation to parody the original.

As with media responses, you should avoid imaginative responses unless you have been taught how to accomplish them.

A significant part of your final grade

Talk is an essential and important part of your Standard Grade course. One third of your final grade comes from your Talk assessments.

Let's see what the Standard Grade Arrangements document says about the assessment of Talk:

For the purposes of assessment, Talking is regarded as falling within one or other of two categories, Discussion and Individual Talk.

Your teacher will decide whether you will be assessed by Discussion or by Individual Talk. There are different Grade Related Criteria for Discussion and Individual Talk.

Group discussions

It cannot be overstressed that every time you are in groups for group discussions you should behave as though the teacher is assessing your group talk skills: you are not necessarily told that assessments are taking place!

The table below shows the difference in the standards expected from Credit level work and General level work across the four areas in which you are assessed.

	Credit	General
Substance and relevance of contribution	Is substantial in quality and relevant to purpose of discussion. Provides a good number of relevant ideas/ responses/ opinions/ experiences. Supports ideas with evidence. Questions and answers relevantly.	Contributes some relevant ideas/ responses/ opinions/experiences **and** EITHER occasionally supports these with evidence/ reasons OR occasionally questions and answers relevantly.
Account taken of other contributions	Takes account of what others have to say in several of the following ways: by analysing/ summarising/ using/ expanding/ supporting/ challenging/ refuting their contributions.	On the whole, takes some account of what others have to say in **one** of the following ways: by summarising/ using/ expanding/ supporting/ challenging their contributions
Awareness of the situation	Behaves in a way appropriate to the situation by: acknowledging the status of chair, leader, interviewer, etc; allowing/ encouraging others to have their say; speaking readily, but not excessively; using language suited to the listener(s).	Behaves in a way appropriate to the situation by **two** of the following; acknowledging the status of chair, leader, interviewer, etc; allowing/ encouraging others to have their say; speaking readily, but not excessively; using language suited to the listener(s).
Control of expression	Is consistently audible and clear and shows some skill in varying intonation to point up meaning and adjusting pace to suit circumstances.	Is largely audible and clear and shows some signs of varying intonation to point up meaning or adjusting pace to suit circumstances.

In group discussions you will probably have no choice in the subject. It may be sprung on you or you may even be unaware that it's a group discussion assessment. You may be given a particular role to play in the group, such as leader, interviewer, reporter. Therefore, it is important to be aware of what is demanded and to be prepared at all times.

Individual talk

If your teacher chooses to assess you by means of an Individual Talk, you need to remember that you will be speaking in front of an audience. The Arrangements state that the audience can consist of a single listener (probably your teacher) or a group, or the whole class.

That means that your talk does *not* have to take place in front of the whole class. You can ask that you be assessed while performing in front of one individual only.

The big difference between Group Discussion and Individual Talk is that:

Individual Talk takes in all forms of talking in which the speaker communicates with minimum response on the part of the listener(s).

But that doesn't mean that you can ignore your audience. When talking in front of an audience, you have to be aware of and respond to their reaction.

First of all, let's look at the GRC to find out *how* you are being assessed for your Individual Talk:

Look out for

Remember that to perform well in a group discussion, you have to make relevant points, be able to agree or challenge successfully, be able to summarise what has been said, and you must, above all, be a good listener.

	Credit	General
Content	Expresses ideas of quality, relevance and interest. Links ideas clearly to each other and to main purpose of task.	Expresses appropriate ideas. Links ideas with some skill.
Purpose (as appropriate)	Conveys information, highlighting what is most significant. Marshals ideas and evidence in support of argument. Gives succinct and coherent account of personal experience, with sensitive expression of feelings and reactions. In storytelling, achieves effect through creative use of structure, tone, timing, vocabulary and characterisation.	Conveys information in an orderly sequence. Orders and presents ideas and opinions with some attempt at reasoning. Gives a reasonably coherent account of a personal experience, expressing feelings and reactions with some sense of involvement. In storytelling, sets the scene, sustains narrative to its climax and conveys some sense of character.
Language	Uses varied and accurate vocabulary. Uses an appropriately wide range of spoken language structures. Uses a register appropriate to topic and audience.	Uses vocabulary and spoken language structure which are largely accurate. Shows some awareness of appropriate register.

Expression	Is consistently fluent. Adjusts pace to suit purpose. Varies intonation to point up meaning.	Is largely audible and clear. Displays some fluency. Shows some signs of ability to vary intonation to point up meaning or to adjust pace to suit the purpose.
Awareness of audience	Takes due account of the requirements and reactions of the audience. Makes appropriate use of eye contact, facial expression and gesture. Requires little or no prompting.	Shows awareness of requirements and reactions of audience. Occasionally makes appropriate use of eye contact, facial expression and gesture. Requires some support through prompting and/or questioning.
Duration	Sustains talk at considerable length, as appropriate to purpose.	Sustains talk at some length, as appropriate to purpose.

Look out for

In group discussion you have to be aware of the contribution made by others. In Individual Talk your skills in communication are much more one way!

There are a number of things you can do to make sure you meet all these requirements:

- First of all, choose a subject in which you are interested and about which you feel strongly, even passionately. The subject can be about something you have experienced.

- If you can, choose an unusual subject, something about which you know a great deal and your audience knows little. That will put you at a considerable advantage.

- Prepare your talk thoroughly. Spend time noting all that you would like to say, but avoid the temptation of writing it out – you are not delivering a spoken essay. In any case, if you try to deliver a spoken essay you can forget what's next and 'freeze' in front of your audience.

- Once you have compiled your notes, shape them into a talk. Make sure your ideas are marshalled in a logical sequence and that they are well-linked. Use evidence to support your argument, but if your talk is about a personal experience, make sure there is interesting detail and that you bear in mind the importance of climax.

- Take time over your introduction – that is what will capture your audience's interest. You almost have to 'woo' them, persuade them that you are worth listening to. Make sure that your introduction has 'signposts' – indications of what your talk is going to be about. And, at all costs, avoid 'I am going to talk about…', a sure way of boring your listener(s).

Look out for

It's best to use headings or bullet points, with maybe each stage of your talk noted on a separate card.

- Use varied vocabulary, varied pitch and intonation, use tone to highlight what is significant, and use the structures of spoken English.

- Be confident – audiences feel comfortable listening to a confident speaker. Pay attention to your body language – don't just stare ahead of you, but make eye contact with your audience. Use facial expressions and hand gestures, but don't overdo them.

▶ Try to use humour. You already know that when you relate an anecdote to your friends or family, you pay attention to the reaction you are getting to your story. You can almost 'feed off' that reaction, adjusting your story as you go along, exaggerating here, pausing there, embellishing the part you played in the story, knowing all the time what will engage their interest and make them laugh. However, don't try too hard to get a laugh.

▶ You must be clear, audible, and fluent. Avoid hesitation, especially the intrusion of 'Um', 'Er', 'Ehh'.

▶ Finally, end effectively. Signpost that you are ending, don't just stop. You could end by summing up or by making a final reflective generalisation.

At some point in your life, you are in all probability going to be asked to give a speech, therefore take the Talk assessment seriously. The skills you acquire here could be among the most useful you ever learn.

Look out for

If it is the whole class that forms your audience, make eye contact with as many actual individuals as you can, a way of making members feel involved.

This book has taken you through the Folio, the Writing paper, the Credit and the General Close Reading papers, and the Talk assessments. You now know what is expected of you in all three areas of assessment: Reading, Writing, and Talk.

You have learned a great deal about grammar, about sentence structure, and about many other language skills needed for Credit and General level work. You know that as you improve your reading skills so you can transfer those to your writing and as your writing skills develop they then can inform your reading skills.

For many candidates the problem is often a poor vocabulary. You must plan to increase it quite considerably for Standard Grade and for Higher, and for later life. It is very sad if you are let down simply because you don't know a few words. Buy yourself a notebook and as you read (try to read an article from a quality newspaper at least twice a week), try to pick out some words you don't know. make a point of finding their meaning and writing them down. You will be surprised at how quickly you extend your vocabulary. If, for example, you know the meaning of the word 'pejorative' (so useful in answering some Close Reading questions), then you could save yourself a great deal of time and effort in trying to express yourself the long way round!

But above all, remember that although this book is dedicated to *improving* your grade, that's not the be-all and end-all. Your mind, your ideas, your life will be improved enormously in quality by reading and by going to the theatre.

Often literature and the theatre challenge our received ideas, the ideas we are brought up with or absorb from family and friends. Literature can confront these ideas, making us rethink them and reflect anew on our attitudes to our experience and the human predicament. But, above all, literature and the theatre are there to be enjoyed.

Don't stop at Standard Grade, don't even stop at Higher... Make literature a central, pivotal part of your life. It will bring you not only much reward and satisfaction, it will give you renewed insight and enrich your entire being.